THE
CEO
FORMULA

Customers. Employees. Owners.

How Profits, Justice, and Vengeance Make or Break Companies

BY

TOM ROLLINS

Copyright © 2020 All Rights Reserved

Table of Contents

Acknowledgments 7
Why I Finally Wrote This Book and Why I Think You Should Read It 8
    Searching for Daylight 10
What is the Point? 11
    Whom Do You Love? 11
    The Puzzle Solves Itself 13
Vast Power Without Purpose 18
    The Early Rule of the Stakes 19
    The Rise of the Shares 20
    Do we have to do it this way? 21
    Trees and Terrorists? Who Deserves a Stake? 24

PROFITS

Looking For Love in All the Wrong Places 30
We Are All Profit-Maximizers Now: A Note on "Surplus" 34
    Everybody MUST be a Winner 37

JUSTICE

Seriously? Profit-Seekers Demand Justice? 42
Customers and Justice 45
    A Note About the Pains and Joys of Self-Awareness 48
Employees and Justice 50
    Doing it Less and Enjoying it More – Bossing Autonomous Beings 52
Owners and Justice 54

VENGEANCE

The Dark Side **58**

The Bitter Taste of Peppercorns **59**

    Partners and Peppercorns: Vengeance in the Laboratory 61

    Customer Vengeance in the Marketplace 62

    Employee Vengeance in the Workplace 64

THE CEO FORMULA

The Obvious Fallacy of Shareholder Supremacy, Customer Supremacy, or Employee Supremacy **70**

The Triumph of CEO **72**

    Corporate Purpose and the "Value Maximization" and Extrusion Nozzle Problems 74

But Wait! There's More. A Lot More. **77**

Who Has a Stake? **80**

    What if everyone had a stake? 81

    Good news and caution about "the good." 82

    How should we define "the good?" 84

    Who gets to decide what is "good?" 89

    Measuring effort is not measuring the "good" 91

    Shortchanging the "good" 92

I See Things That Never Were and Say, "Why Not?" And They Say, "Here's Why Not." **96**

    Business as Applied Science 97

    Accounting Precision in Perspective 99

    Massively Misaligned Incentives 101

    Ramming Speed, Scotty! 107

Concluding Thoughts on Who We Become in a World of Reciprocity. 108

A Case Study:
How CEO Worked for Our Company

Creating CEO Goals 114

    Climbing Towards the Goals 117

    Extreme Action to Create Extreme Customer Satisfaction 118

    Creating a Rich Culture of Custom and Practice for Your People ... 120

All This and You're Still in Kansas? Right? 123

Why did I wait so long to write this? 124

Bibliography 126

About the Author 134

THE CEO FORMULA

Acknowledgments

To thank everyone individually who shaped the ideas in this book would double its length. Thus, I hope that my former colleagues at The Teaching Company will understand if I thank all of them rather than single out a few for having collaborated to build a company as beautiful as our courses. I must rely on the same principle to thank the hundreds of teachers and professors who were the incarnate ideal I had imagined when I started The Teaching Company.

For their willingness to review and critique drafts of my original article and then this book, I am deeply indebted to Eric Andersen, Frederick Reichheld, Robert Shrum, Lawrence Summers, Timothy Taylor, and William White. For his expert guidance in actually publishing this book, I thank Scott Blair. And for the pact to complete long-postponed goals, I thank Rob Serraino.

Many authors thank their families for their indulgence while a book was being born. I owe mine that and more. For her patient and flawless reviews of an embarrassing number of drafts, I thank my marvelous wife, Vicki. And I thank my children Tom and Kay for their editorial and research assistance.

This crew steered me clear of many errors and towards many opportunities and challenges. For mistakes in fact and emphasis, I alone am to blame. The anxiety that I suspect most authors feel as their ideas leave the private page and are launched in to the wild is overwhelmed by my gratitude to those who helped me bring this book into being.

Why I Finally Wrote This Book and Why I Think You Should Read It

My book describes a uniquely powerful way to restructure a company to create more – many times more – value for its customers, employees, and owners. I sincerely believe that if the "CEO Formula" were followed, it would create greater wealth, reduce inequality in incomes, make capitalism more humane, ethically driven, and popular. Capitalism needs all of that, especially today. A disclaimer: My argument is rooted in the hard facts of profit and loss, not moral assertions, though I relish the irony that hard facts show that certain moral behaviors are heavily rewarded economically.

I've been thinking about these issues since 1996 when the company I founded in 1989 – The Teaching Company, also known as The Great Courses – was in sufficient trouble that it needed to be restructured from the ground up. As someone once said: "Never waste a crisis."

This part of my book has been difficult to write. It compels me to recall and re-live some of the agony – and the joy – of creating a new company from scratch. It requires me to remember that I was terrible at running a business until I'd been at it for six years and, as the Alcoholics say, "hit bottom" in a way that forced me to change my company and myself. And then, as you'll see, I have written some arguably patronizing paragraphs about what you should do and how you will feel. Those sentences wouldn't write themselves without direct address to the reader, so please forgive their pushy nature.

And then there's the bragging about our results. It is true that I'm very proud of what my team accomplished at The Teaching Company. But I also believe that I owe it to you – especially if you read my book – to provide some proof that what I advocate actually worked, even if it entails some "flexing."[1]

---

[1] A quick data-point. From an initial and sole investment of $1.7 million, The Teaching Company grew to be worth 90 times that much in 17 years. The CEO Formula worked. Big flex.

I believe that CEO Formula can create a great deal of wealth for others, maybe even for you. So, if I may ask for a modest reciprocal exchange, please hold your temptation to be impatient as you read my tale of woe and triumph.

August 23, 1996 was the worst day of my professional life. My company was six years old, and had tripled revenues in three years, from $3 million to $9 million. Every part of our vessel now moaned under the strain; old processes couldn't handle the volume; "battlefield promotions" had landed many folks in jobs over their heads; firefighting was our most lauded function, and so on. The story is familiar at fast-growing start-ups.

I founded The Teaching Company, which produces audio and video courses taught by the best professors in the country in 1990. It was and is a great idea – and at the time, that's all I thought I needed. The news that things were in a bad way came when we summarized our first customer satisfaction survey results. I had received so many "love letters" from customers that I had developed a blind spot for the unhappiness we were creating, too. Only 51% of our customers rated their satisfaction with the company at the top of a satisfaction scale. In 1996, I hired a consulting firm to assess the company and help us prepare for yet more rapid growth. Part of their effort included confidential surveys of my employees.

The August 23rd briefing on their survey was excruciating. Especially to our managers, the company's goals seemed unattainable, there were too many priorities, hiring practices were so ad hoc that they were rated less than 4 out of 10, and our plan for growth was only one point better. Many people were overwhelmed, confused, and bitter. My illusions about the invigorating quality of working in a hard-charging, fast-changing workplace led by me were served back bitter and cold.

Their report on that awful Friday changed my company. I sensed these problems coming; the intensity floored me. It was time for me to play to my strengths.

Searching for Daylight

Before starting my company, I spent eight years in high school and college as a competitive debater.[2] Hitting the library in search of the best evidence I could find was my default solution for problems. I had also worked as a lawyer and as the lead staffer on a U.S. Senate Committee creating policy and statutes.[3] This last job required a deep understanding of how voters feel and behave. I won't say that I had such an understanding, but I certainly tried to achieve it. My need to understand my customers was even more urgent.

With my company practically in flames, I threw myself into figuring out what makes businesses succeed and why. I bought and read the entire first-year curriculum of the Harvard Business School, roughly a three-foot shelf of case studies and teaching notes. I read the business classics and what I believed to be the hot new literature. Over months, I covered the walls of my apartment with post-it notes, diagrams on sheets of legal paper, and makeshift posters. I spent a day consulting with the legendary Jim Collins, who, to my good fortune, was a very loyal customer of The Teaching Company. The company's goal to "ignite the passion for the life of the mind" was a phrase Jim developed while working with me. I assembled a dozen people from across the company to meet every Wednesday afternoon for months to work through what our company should – and could – become.

---

[2] William Southworth, The Decade's Best in College Debate, Journal of the American Speech Association, Fall 1981. https://groups.wfu.edu/NDT/Articles/1970s.html

[3] Edward M. Kennedy Histories, Thomas M. Rollins Oral History, (The University of Virginia, The Miller Center, March, April, May 12, May 14, 2009) https://millercenter.org/the-presidency/presidential-oral-histories/thomas-m-rollins-oral-history-032009-chief-counsel. (accessed November 30, 2019).

What is the Point?

When I waded into the literature, data, and our immediate problems, I was reminded of Nietzsche's aphorism that "the most fundamental form of human stupidity is forgetting what we are trying to do in the first place." The more I read, the more I thought that business had an even more fundamental problem: No one had actually <u>forgotten</u> what business was trying to do in the first place because we'd <u>never agreed</u> on what businesses were supposed to do.

The world of business, after all these years, was – and is – surprisingly unclear or simply misguided about its own purpose. "Maximizing shareholder value" is still the orthodox description of the primary or sole purpose of a shareholder-owned firm. Yet we know intuitively and empirically that this is wrong. Intuitively, we know that fools can – and, empirically, many do – maximize shareholder value by diluting product quality, gaming prices, cutting compensation to employees, or by buying back company shares at high prices to boost them further. The fallacy of following this Scrooge-like logic of contempt for other contributors to a firm's value becomes evident when customers and workers migrate to other firms. The paradox is that making a firm's primary purpose the maximization of shareholder returns will reduce those returns. The pathbreaking book Built to Last by Jim Collins and Jerry Porras summarized the remarkable evidence I'll describe in more detail later: "Shattered Myth #3: The most successful companies exist first and foremost to maximize profits…..[T]he visionary companies make more money than the more purely profit-driven comparison companies."[4]

Whom Do You Love?

But if increasing shareholder value isn't the purpose of the firm – or even the best way to increase shareholder value – what is?

---

[4] James Collins and Jerry Porras, Built to Last: Successful Habits of Visionary Companies (New York: Harper Collins Publishers, 1994), 8.

I scoured the literature for months. It wasn't as though I took a sabbatical. I just spent every minute out of the office researching my questions on how best to build our company. (Being single at the time helped.)

And I've written in the main body of this book how the answers play out, so I won't repeat them here except in summary. Prioritizing shareholder gains produced weaker performance for shareholders. I clearly saw evidence that companies that had prioritized satisfying their customers had done far better, especially for owners. The same was true of companies that had prioritized their employees. The causal link between shareholder primacy and company success appeared to be the weakest.

The problem is that sole focus on any of customers, employees, or owners by themselves is logically and financially absurd if taken to its maximizing conclusion. Let me underscore the cardinal lessons I learned.

- Shareholders will do best in the short run if product quality is diluted and salaries are cut, or if productive investments are foregone so the company can buy back its own shares and inflate its share price. This may improve results in the short run, but it will damage a firm's long-term value as customers and employees leave and as short-term owners harvest their profits and go elsewhere, like locusts.

- Customers will prosper in the short run if product quality is vastly enhanced and prices are set near zero. An old Dilbert cartoon quotes Ratbert: "We have new market research to show that customers want product quality to be greatly increased and everything should be free."

- Employee as King? Most managers know that a firm run solely for its Employees cannot last. Pushed to its logical and financial extreme, we could create a happy workplace for Homer Simpson in a La-Z-Boy with a pile of donuts handy, but no investor would park money there and no customer would buy whatever Homer does or makes, though Homer might be extremely satisfied. Some dot.com era excesses come to mind.

Fundamental questions were not answered by logic or examples. What mechanism caused the success of some companies that had emphasized customers and employees rather than apply the orthodox rule to prioritize shareholders? And what limiting principle could prevent the disastrous entailments of Scrooge owners, Ratbert customers, and Homer Simpson employees?

As I searched, pieces came together.

I had the good fortune to stumble on *The Economics of Strategy*[5] which showed the competitive uses of Consumer surplus. It made clear that Customers were in the profit-maximizing game, too. It was a baby step to see how the same idea applied to Employees.

But I still couldn't really understand the mechanism that led Customers and Employees to treat companies well or to abandon them so quickly when a company short-changed them.

The missing piece was somewhere I wasn't looking.

For two decades, I was constantly in the hunt for better sales and marketing strategies. I've read some classics that made my company much more successful. But I hit strategic paydirt when I found and read Professor Robert Cialdini's deeply surprising book, *Influence: The Psychology of Persuasion*. He reported on the power of reciprocity in human exchanges. He had data that were hard to believe until its cumulative impact left no room for doubt. That was the missing explanation I'd been searching to find. Customers and employees will reciprocate generosity from a company partly because we are all profit-maximizers, but also because we are all hard-wired to encourage pro-social economic behavior and to punish those who do not share created value.

The Puzzle Solves Itself

The final proof, the cumulative summary of the evidence I'd found, what the law would call "clear and convincing" proof, was in *Product Juggernauts* by Deschamp and Ryanak of Arthur D. Little. They summarized and charted the data unearthed by Professors Kotter and Heskett in 1992.

As you'll see in the main text, the Kotter and Heskett study was a comparison of three groups of companies: one group focused primarily or exclusively on creating value for Owners, another primarily on

---

[5] David Besanko, David Dranove, and Mark Shanley, "Competitive Advantage and Value Creation: Analytical Tools and Conceptual Foundations," The Economics of Strategy, (New York: John Wiley & Sons, 1996), Chapter 12.

Customers and Employees, and a third gave high but equal attention to creating value for all three. Here is the data:

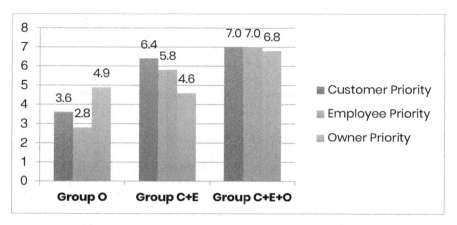

The results after 11 years were a new world-view. Over an 11-year period, firms placing a high emphasis on creating value for owners produced a baseline value of X. Firms that placed a high priority on creating value for customers and employees produced returns of almost 200% of X. But firms that placed high priority on all three – Customers, Employees, and Owners ("CEO") – created a return 700% higher than the firms whose primary focus was on Owners. Thus, those who sought only to please their owners did the worst job. C+E+O trumps O. Massively.

Here is a replica of the graphic summarizing the Kotter and Heskett study. I showed this to every Employee at my company and it was part of the "welcome interview" for every new Employee.

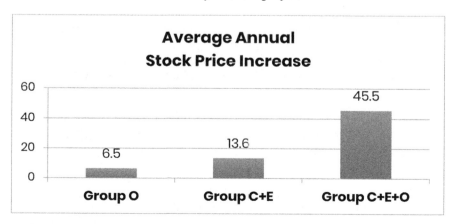

After months of searching, the puzzle had solved itself. I'll briefly summarize the problem and its solution here.

There are now two dominant and connected ideas on how a company should be structured and run that are destroying the value that companies should be creating. The first dominant and destructive idea is that the primary purpose of a corporation is to create maximum profits for its shareholders, its owners. I show that this idea is, in practice, counterproductive because it <u>reduces</u> value for shareholders by ignoring the sources of value a company creates.

The second dominant and destructive idea is that the way to maximize profits for shareholders is by capturing as much profit as possible in every exchange with its customers and employees. I show how both ideas are – forgive the term – intellectually "bankrupt." The argument against the dominant views below matches the titles of the main sections of the book.

1. <u>Profits</u>: Customers and employees, as well as owners, ("CEO") are <u>also</u> profit-maximizers, just like the company. All companies do the same two things: they make things and sell them. The employees do all the making and customers do all the buying. Owners provide capital to launch or expand companies, but they are not the sustaining engine of value creation.

2. <u>Justice</u>: C, E, and O <u>all demand reciprocity</u> – a fair equivalent to their contributions to the company – in exchanges with a company. Our instinctive insistence for reciprocity appears to be built in to our social DNA. Violating the dominant rules, some companies reciprocally share value with C, E, and O and, as a result, customers buy more and more often, employees work harder and smarter, owners are more patient with their increasingly valuable capital, and these firms flourish, massively out-performing their rivals. (The data here are stunning, even inspiring.)

3. <u>Vengeance</u>: If a firm follows the orthodox view and does not share what C, E, and O regard as a reciprocally fair equivalent to their contributions to the firm, the firm will underperform, wither, and possibly die.

4. <u>The CEO Formula</u>: Simply: there are three groups with which a company is engaged in reciprocal creation of value: its customers, employees, and owners. A company should confer profit to these three groups to the extent that they will confer more profit back to the company – the company must profit

reciprocally, too, or it will fail to create as much value with its resources as it should.

The CEO Formula is self-regulating. The need for mutual value-creation prevents wasteful distributions of a company's gains that could be used to create greater value. And the need to create value for all three groups checks any one group from harvesting more than its share of the firm's value. I show extensive evidence that sharing mutually created value with customers and employees will create significant – even dramatic – increases in value for the company and for all three partners. And I show that <u>all</u> three groups, including owners, must receive high and equal priority for the CEO Formula to work.

I also explain why one response to the dominant shareholder view – so-called "stakeholder" theory and its companion "Corporate Social Responsibility" – is mistaken and why there are only three legitimate stakeholders in a company: customers, employees, and owners.

Because I am refuting a couple of dominant ideologies in business and microeconomic thought, I have laid out my argument very carefully. For many readers, some steps may seem obvious, or, at best, over-proven. (Really? Finnish dentists?) I hope you'll be patient with the exposition even if you hurry through some sections. I have written with the most care I can muster, and, as a result, may seem windy when I just want to make sure that my arguments take nothing for granted.

So, here is what I hope will be my gift to you. Your reciprocal contribution, should you accept the gift, will be to read and apply the results of my labors.

Tom Rollins
January 2020
McLean, Virginia

Vast Power Without Purpose

"Hegel predicted that the basic unit of modern society would be the state, Marx that it would be the commune, Lenin and Hitler that it would be the political party. Before that, a succession of saints and sages claimed the same for the parish church, the feudal manor, and the monarchy....

[T]hey have all been proved wrong. The most important organization in the world is the company: the basis of prosperity in the West and the best hope for the future of the rest of the world."

- John Micklethwait and Adrian Wooldridge, The Company, 2005

"The limited liability corporation is the greatest single discovery of modern times. Even steam and electricity are less important than the limited liability company."

- Nicholas Murray Butler, president of Columbia University and winner of the Nobel Peace Prize, 1911

The company may be the most powerful social unit other than the family and the state.[6] And the modern company was almost certainly a necessary precondition for the success of the Industrial Revolution, which has increased the human standard of living 100-fold.[7] Most of us

---

[6] "This new 'corporation' . . . was the first autonomous institution in hundreds of years, the first to create a power center that was in society yet independent of the central government of the national state." Peter F. Drucker, *The Frontiers of Management*, 1987 (Abingdon, U.K.: Routledge, Reprint 2012), 170.

[7] Steven Pinker, *Enlightenment Now: The Case for Reason, Science, Humanism, and Progress* (London: Penguin Books, 2019), 81.

will spend a huge plurality of the waking hours of our lives working for companies. And virtually everything that surrounds us – houses, plates, cars, buildings, railroads, electricity, cellphone signals, food, and on and on – was made by a company.

We would expect that by now we'd have decided what companies are for. And we'd be wrong.

The purpose of a company is still vigorously contested. The struggle is between two camps: those who say that the sole purpose of a corporation is to create value for its shareholders and those who argue that its purpose is to create value for its "stakeholders," which can include many parties, such as customers, employees, and a host of others as we'll see shortly.

Shares vs. Stakes.

In this debate, we all have a stake: The foundations of our economy and prosperity depend on how this conflict is resolved. I will argue that both camps are wrong, that many businesses can become far more valuable, and that we can create an enormous amount of wealth for society at large if we understand the proper purposes of a company.[8]

The Early Rule of the Stakes

For much of the history of the modern company, the stakeholder theory of corporate purpose was dominant – the company should serve the interests of its "stakeholders," only one category of which should be its shareholders. Though it is a distinctly minority view today, the stakeholder theory was dominant in the post-World War II economy. In a 1961 survey of 1700 executives by the Harvard Business Review, 83% of those executives agreed that "[f]or corporation executives to act in the interests of shareholders alone, and not also in the interests of employees and consumers, is unethical."[9] Indeed, one firebrand said in 1951 that

---

[8] Throughout, I will use the terms "company," "corporation," and "firm" as interchangeable synonyms. There are distinctions, but, in the context of this book, those are not differences.

[9] Raymond C. Baumhart, "How Ethical Are Businessmen?," *Harvard Business Review* (July-August 1961), 6, 10.

"the job of management is to maintain an equitable and working balance among the claims of various directly interested groups...stockholders, employees, customers, and the public at large."[10] The author? A radical in the pre-Twitter era? No. Frank Abrams, the Chairman of Standard Oil of New Jersey, the great oligopoly that provoked the passage of the first antitrust laws.

The Rise of the Shares

But then something happened. The shareholder camp received its strongest modern expression from Nobel Prize-winning economist Milton Friedman in the *New York Times* on September 13, 1970. The title of the article says it all: "The social responsibility of business is to increase its profits." And, in the article itself, he argues that ". . . there is one and only one social responsibility of business – to use its resources and engage in activities designed to increase its profits so long as it stays in the rules of the game, which is to say, engages in open and free competition, without deception or fraud."

When Friedman published his argument that only shareholder interests matter, it was, according to Columbia Law School Professor Jeffrey N. Gordon, "a *scandale* because of its unvarnished emphasis on the shareholder value as virtually the sole criterion on which corporate performance should be judged."[11] The *Economist* recalls that many were "shocked" by Friedman's forthrightness.[12]

> **The Economist recalls that many were "shocked" by Friedman's forthrightness.**

---

[10] Michael Lind as cited in Walter Kiechel, "The Management Century," *Harvard Business Review* (November 2012), https://hbr.org/2012/11/the-management-century (accessed November 30, 2019).

[11] Jeffrey N. Gordon, "The Rise of Independent Directors in the United States, 1950-2005: Of Shareholder Value and Stock Market Prices," *Stanford Law Review* 59 (April 2010), www.jstor.org/stable/40040395 (accessed November 30, 2019), 1520.

[12] *The Economist*, August 24, 2019, 15

Shocking or not, beginning in the 1980s, several factors enabled Friedman's view to prevail. Among those factors was the rise of hostile takeovers that often punished management teams – with unemployment – for failing to improve stock prices.

Management and boards of directors reacted. In addition to creating legal bulwarks against takeovers, management teams focused on increasing stock prices. And to ensure that management's incentives aligned with those of shareholders, management compensation was increasingly tied by directors to increases in share prices. Thus, writes Professor Gordon, "by the end of the 1990s, the triumph of the shareholder value criterion was nearly complete."[13] The late Cornell Law School Professor Lynn Stout concurred that the dominant – almost exclusive – view was now that companies exist to maximize the gains of shareholders. "[B]y the turn of the millennium...business and policy elites in the United States and much of the rest of the world as well accepted as a truth that should not be questioned that corporations exist to maximize shareholder value."[14] And now, as of 2017, 48.5% of all CEO pay at the 500 largest American corporations is in stock.[15] At the 200 largest public firms in 2014, 72% of CEO pay was in stock and share buybacks.[16]

Do we have to do it this way?

The shareholder view is not required by law. No state statute that grants charters to corporations specifies profit maximization as the goal of those

---

[13] Gordon, "Independent Directors," 1530.

[14] Lynn Stout, *The Shareholder Value Myth: How Putting Shareholders First Harms Investors, Corporations, and the Public* (San Francisco: Berrett-Koehler, 2013), 4.

[15] Equilar, CEO Pay Trends, 2018 https://marketing.equilar.com/43-2018-ceo-pay-trends.

[16] William A. Galston and Elaine C. Kamarck, "More builders and fewer traders: a growth strategy for the American economy," *The Brookings Institution,* June 2015, https://www.brookings.edu/wp-content/uploads/2016/06/CEPMGlastonKarmarck4.pdf (accessed November 30, 2019).

given legal authority to start and operate a company. Most often, states allow a chartered company to pursue any "legitimate business purpose."[17]

Delaware, where most of the country's largest corporations are incorporated, has the largest say on legitimate corporate purpose. In 1985, the Delaware Supreme Court held in *Unocal Corp. v. Mesa Petroleum* that directors of a corporation may, in making business decisions, consider "the impact on 'constituencies' other than shareholders (*i.e.*, creditors, customers, employees, and perhaps even the community generally)."[18]

To be clear, shareholders in publicly traded companies are not synonymous with the common usage of the term "owners." Ownership implies complete control over a piece of property. I own my tennis racket and can hit tennis balls with it, sell it, destroy it, or paint it blue. Shareholders, by contrast, are parties to a contract with a corporation under which they have limited rights. They own "shares," which is not the same as being overlords of a company. Their only genuine power is to vote for the Board of Directors of the corporation, and, in the case of non-voting shares, not even that. Shareholders cannot select or fire the CEO, they cannot award themselves dividends or even cut back on a fleet of lavish private jets. They are entitled to income from the company if the company decides to share some of it with them. And they can sell their shares to someone else, which they may well want to do if those shares have become more valuable while they owned them.

This is in no way a diminution of the importance of shareholders in a company's responsibilities. Shares are purchased with savings, and companies are stewards of those savings, often vital retirement savings: "72% of the value of all domestically held stocks is owned by pension plans, 401(k)s and individual retirement accounts, or held by life insurance companies to fund annuities and death benefits."[19] As I will

---

[17] Stout, *The Shareholder Value Myth*, 28.

[18] *Unocal Corp. v. Mesa Petroleum Co.*, 493 A.2d 946 (Del. 1985). The commonly cited case for the shareholder view is *Revlon v. MacAndrews & Forbes Holdings* 506 A.2d 173 (Del. 1986), a narrow exception to the business judgment rule in which the court held that when a company has decided to put itself up for sale it must put the interests of shareholders first and accept an offer from the highest bidder.

[19] Phil Gramm and Mike Solon, "Warren's Assault on Retiree Wealth," *The Wall Street Journal*, September 10, 2019,

argue throughout, the company has opportunities with and obligations to shareholders. When I use the term "owners" in this book, I am referring to shareholders.[20]

Recently, the stakeholder camp has mounted a resurgence on behalf of many, many interests other than shareholders. Senator Warren's "Accountable Capitalism Act" would require all companies with more than $1 billion in annual tax receipts to be chartered by the federal government and then charged to "create a general public benefit."[21] The bill also imposes on directors a duty to consider the interests of shareholders, employees (including of subsidiaries and suppliers), customers, the community, the local and global environment, "community and societal factors," and "the long-term."[22] Another section requires that 40% of votes for board seats be cast by workers.[23] The Senator would also require all corporations to be federally licensed, and licenses could be revoked if companies failed to satisfy federal authorities about their governance and use of profits.[24] These decisions about license revocation would, of course, be made by government employees who may or may not have any experience or expertise in operating a business or even an organization.

Senators Schumer and Sanders would require companies to provide wages of at least $15 per hour, seven days of paid sick leave, and "decent

---

https://www.wsj.com/articles/warrens-assault-on-retiree-wealth-11568155283 (accessed November 30, 2019)

[20] Why not use the word shareholders instead? As you have probably anticipated, I will detail the "CEO Formula" shortly and the acronym CEO would be less resonant for business people if it were CES. At my company, we created our system before I'd seen the much more clever CEO acronym, so ours was a formula for "Customers, Investors, and People" or "CIP," pronounced "chip." Investor is a much closer synonym for shareholders than "owners."

[21] S. 3348, 115th Congress (2017-2018), Section 5 (b)(2), https://www.congress.gov/bill/115th-congress/senate-bill/3348/text.

[22] Ibid., 5(c).

[23] Ibid, 6(b).

[24] Elizabeth Warren, "Issues," https://elizabethwarren.com/issues#rebuild-the-middle-class (accessed November 30, 2019).

pensions and reliable health benefits" or else companies would lose the ability to buy their own shares and possibly even to distribute dividends, effectively forbidding companies to share any of their profits with their shareholders unless they meet the two Senators' thresholds for employee pay and benefits.[25]

Others have suggested that customer supremacy should be the new rule. Professor Roger Martin argued in the *Harvard Business Review* in 2010 that shareholders should be knocked off their pedestal and customers should be the primary focus of value-creation by a business, marking "The Age of Customer-Driven Capitalism."[26]

Trees and Terrorists?
Who Deserves a Stake?

So, if the stakeholder camp is rising, our first question should be "who is a 'stakeholder?'" Here, scholarly and legal reflection is murky, edging to the bizarre. Most simply, as some of the current reasoning goes, anyone who affects or is affected by the actions of a company has a stake in its behavior. Senator Warren's bill, for example, requires a company's directors to balance the "pecuniary interest of the shareholders ... with the best interests of persons that are materially affected by the conduct of the ... corporation."[27] Thus, applying the test that all who are "materially affected" by a company have a stake in it, customers, employees, owners, the community, "societal factors,"[28] the state, and, perhaps, even

---

[25] Charles Schumer and Bernard Sanders, "Schumer and Sanders: Limit Corporate Stock Buybacks," *The New York Times*, February 4, 2019, https://www.nytimes.com/2019/02/03/opinion/chuck-schumer-bernie-sanders.html (accessed November 30, 2019).

[26] Roger Martin, "The Age of Customer Capitalism," *Harvard Business Review*, January-February 2010 https://hbr.org/2010/01/the-age-of-customer-capitalism (accessed November 30, 2019).

[27] S. 3348, Section 5(c)(1)(a)(ii).

[28] Ibid.

nonhumans[29] and, in one extreme logical extension, terrorists[30] have been identified as potential stakeholders deserving a voice if not a vote in a company's governance.

One set of scholars identifies the following among stakeholders: Latent stakeholders – which includes Dormant, Discretionary, and Demanding stakeholders – as well as Expectant Stakeholders – which includes Dominant, Dependent, and Dangerous stakeholders.[31] In this case, cute academic taxonomy has triumphed over common business sense. Good luck to any company in trying to figure out for whom they are working if all these claimants must be served!

This murkiness in the stakeholder camp is surely one of the reasons that the shareholder camp has continued to prevail. Whatever may be its limitations, giving absolute priority to a company's shareholders has the benefit of ruthless clarity in telling managers and directors what to do. As Michael Jensen of Harvard Business School has argued, "stakeholder theory directs corporate managers to serve 'many masters.' And, to paraphrase the old adage, when there are many masters, all end up being shortchanged. . . . companies embracing stakeholder theory will experience managerial confusion, conflict, inefficiency, and perhaps even competitive failure."[32]

Stakeholder theory has reached nothing approaching consensus on clear, coherent, and sensible means to decide who has a worthy stake. And even if such consensus could be reached, stakeholder advocates may still lack clear guidance on how to serve each of the stakeholders identified. There are, on this planet, always trade-offs. How much of our annual spending should go to improving the quality of products for customers, increasing

---

[29] Mark Starik, "Should Trees Have Managerial Standing? Toward Shareholder Status for Nonhuman Nature," 14 *Journal of Business Ethics* (March 1995).

[30] R. Edward Freeman, *Strategic Management: A Stakeholder Approach* (Cambridge: Cambridge University Press, 2010), 53.

[31] Ronald K. Mitchell, Bradley R. Agle, and Donna J. Wood, "Toward a Theory of Stakeholder Identification and Salience: Defining the Principle of Who and What Really Counts," *The Academy of Management Review* 22 (1997), 853-86.

[32] Michael Jensen, "Value Maximization, Stakeholder Theory, and the Corporate Objective Function," *Journal of Applied Corporate Finance*, Fall 2001, 9.

compensation to employees, distributing profits to owners, or to improving local schools? The more you do of one, the less you can do of others. Stakeholder advocates must prescribe a means to prioritize various stakeholders or the school of thought only generates lists signifying nothing.

It may strike us as somewhat astonishing that centuries after corporations were first chartered, we have not decided what they are for.[33] Without conviction on this issue, how can they be run or regulated? We are reminded of Nietzsche's aphorism that "the most fundamental form of human stupidity is forgetting what we are trying to do in the first place." So what are we trying to do?

---

[33] That comment should be qualified. Chartered corporations were originally created by royal governments to exploit the discoveries and efficiencies of routes to trade with the New World and Asia. Companies were granted monopolies over given areas in exchange for a government share in the profits. Thus: "The Hudson's Bay Company," "The Virginia Company," and "The Company of Distant Parts." John Micklethwait and Adrian Wooldridge, *The Company: A Short History of a Revolutionary Idea* (London: Orion Publishing Group, 2005), 17.

PROFITS

Looking For Love in All the Wrong Places

> *"You know something. What you know you can't explain. But you feel it; you've felt it your entire life...that there's something wrong with the world. You don't know what it is, but it's there, like a splinter in your mind, driving you mad."*
>
> — Morpheus to Neo in *The Matrix*

Here's the thing we know that we can't explain: Strong emphasis on shareholders <u>reduces</u> the value created for shareholders. Consider this somewhat overwhelming "data point" from the classic *Built to Last* by Jim Collins and Jerry Porras. Among several comparisons Collins and Porras make between 18 pairs of "visionary" and "comparison" companies – carefully matched pairs observed from 1926 to 1990 – is that visionary companies were dramatically less likely than their counterparts to place primary emphasis on shareholders or profits. Of 18 comparison companies, 7 of 18 were highly profit- or shareholder-oriented; <u>not one of the visionaries was</u>. Visionaries placed a <u>lower emphasis on profits</u> and shareholders in 12 of 18 cases, <u>two-thirds of the time</u>. Did failure to prioritize shareholders hurt shareholders?

Brace yourself: Over the observed period, $1 invested in the visionary companies returned $6,356; in the comparison companies, $995. The comparison companies were not weaklings – they roughly doubled the return of the market as a whole, which is very hard to do; they had to be twice as good as average public company managers. Visionaries, departing sharply from shareholder primacy, produced returns <u>15 times greater</u> than the market for their shareholders.[34]

---

[34] James Collins and Jerry Porras, *Built to Last: Successful Habits of Visionary Companies* (New York: Harper Collins Publishers, 1994), 284.

That's very hard to reconcile with the now-dominant mandate to create value only for shareholders.

Another study, covering a mere 11-year time span, offers insight into the causes of shareholder primacy's failure to serve shareholders. Professors Kotter and Heskett of Harvard Business School reported in 1992 on a comparison of 200 companies divided into three groups: one group focused primarily or exclusively on creating value for owners, another on creating value primarily for customers and employees, and a third gave high but equal attention to creating value for all three. The study tracked the increase in market value of each group.

The results were astonishing. I repeat here their discovery from the introduction. Over an 11-year period, firms placing a high emphasis on creating value for owners produced a baseline value of X for their owners. Firms that placed a high priority on creating value for customers and employees produced returns of almost 200% of X. But firms that placed high priority on all three – customers, employees, and owners ("CEO") – created a return 700% higher for their owners than the firms whose primary focus was on Owners. Thus, those who sought only to please their Owners did the worst job for them of the three groups. C+E+O trumps O. Massively.[35] That is the "C.E.O. Formula."

> **C+E+O trumps O. Massively.**
> **That is the "C.E.O. Formula."**

From here on, I will capitalize Customers, Employees, and Owners.

---

[35] John Kotter and James Heskett, *Corporate Culture and Performance* (New York: Free Press, 1992), 4; Jean-Phillippe Deschamps and Ranganath Nayak, *Product Juggernauts: How Companies Mobilize to Generate a Stream of Market Winners* (Boston: Harvard Business School Press, 1995), 6.

THE CEO FORMULA

Here is the data as charted by Deschamps and Nayak of Arthur D. Little Inc.

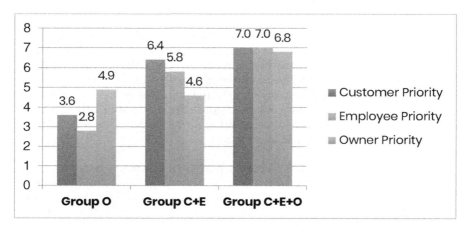

And here are the increase in values of these three groups after 11 years.

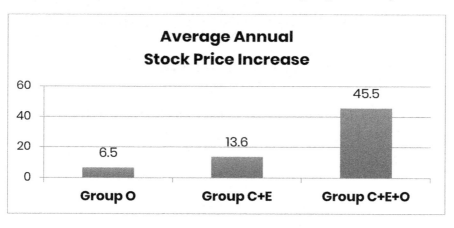

Here is the splinter in the mind of shareholder primacy: It doesn't work for shareholders. Collins and Porras call shareholder primacy "Shattered Myth #3: The most successful companies exist first and foremost to maximize profits.....[T]he visionary companies make more money than the more purely profit-driven comparison companies."[36]

---

[36] Collins and Porras, *Built to Last*, 8.

How can this be? How is it that by working to serve three constituencies, companies produced greater Owner value than if they had focused only on Owners? Doesn't this contradict the principle and value of shareholder primacy? Doesn't this contradict the claim that a firm can only pursue one goal successfully? Isn't this beginning to look as though shareholder primacy might be as silly as stakeholding terrorists? Are both camps missing something?

We have a paradox on our hands; by pursuing the interests of Customers and Employees as well as Owners, Owners benefit more than if they are the primary or exclusive object of corporate purpose.

By resolving this paradox – that creating value for all three groups creates more value for each of them than if any one of them were central – many businesses could greatly increase the value they create for their Owners. And their Customers. And their Employees. Allow me to explain why with two important premises:

- One, we – Customers, Employees, Owners, and companies – all seek "profits." The next chapter on surplus explains this premise, though it may well be obvious to many. Good.
- Two, we demand justice from other economic actors. The chapters on "justice" establish this premise theoretically and empirically.
- It is because of these two premises that both the shareholder and stakeholder camps have failed.37

---

37 A note about "suppliers" – people or companies who provide materials, components, or even traditionally interior functions of a company, such as quality control, but which have been outsourced. Many regard suppliers as a separate species of stakeholder. I do not. The company buying goods or services from a supplier is a <u>Customer</u>. The principles that govern Company : Customer relations are the same as those that govern Supplier : Company relations.

Shortly, I'll show how customers and companies divide the profit made by a customer's purchase. In this business-to-business context, I will venture that the division of surplus between company and Customer is much more carefully calculated by the Customer than in the business-to-consumer context. Companies deploy spreadsheets to calculate the costs and benefits of a supplier relationship; consumers are usually less disciplined, though their rough internal algorithms and instincts for fairness can produce high quality answers.

It is also possible to think of suppliers as Employees but supplier relationships are both more closed and more open than Employee

We Are All Profit-Maximizers Now: A Note on "Surplus"

What follows immediately is a brief, basic description of capitalism at the "micro" level, where firms and their resources interact.[38] I'm doing so to show the root mechanics of production and exchange so we can see later that Customers and Employees – that's all of us – are doing the same thing as profit-seeking companies.

Perhaps the simplest equation in business is R – C = P. Revenue (or, its synonym, Sales) minus Costs equals Profit (or Earnings, or Income).

Here is a simpler version of the rule for all of us: if you spend more than you make, you are generating losses. Same rule for business: If revenue ("R") is less than cost ("C"), a firm is generating losses.

Unless a money-losing firm turns that around and reduces costs to less than revenue or increases revenue without proportionately increasing costs, it will eventually go out of business because it will run out of money. The only question is how long it will take. If the firm started out with a lot of money in the bank or has other assets it can convert to cash

---

relationships. Employment relationships are more open in the sense that duties and roles are more loosely defined than in a supplier relationship where all exchanges are usually defined by contract. And employment relationships are less open because they are governed by labor laws that may, for example, make it more difficult or expensive to end an employment relationship than to terminate a supplier.

[38] I describe "ideal" capitalism. By "ideal," I mean simply that there are not monopoly conditions, forced labor, fraud, or competition based on who is best at evading laws and regulations.

to pay the costs that its revenues can't cover, it will eat through those assets and then go bankrupt.

This is Adam Smith's "Invisible Hand" at work. Pity whoever put up their money in the money-losing firm's bank account; they will likely lose it all. (They might get something back in bankruptcy when the firm has to sell everything to pay people off at dimes or pennies on the dollar.) But, if the firm has to tell the truth that it has costs higher than revenues, no one else will give them money. Banks won't loan because they risk not getting paid back.[39] Investors won't put their hard-won savings at risk in exchange for shares of stock in the company because those will likely be worthless – the firm makes no profit, so it will not be able to distribute profits to its shareholders. (There are huge exceptions to this obvious rule. One is when a firm generates short-term losses to grow rapidly, and having grown enough, will stop losing money and start generating profits. Amazon over the past 20 years is a good example. Another is a start-up drug-development firm trying to create new cancer checkpoint inhibitors. It will often show losses for quite a while because research and development is an investment in future earnings.)

Channeling new investment is a key power of Smith's Invisible Hand. Society's limited supply of savings that can be used by firms will flow away from firms that consume more value than they create and towards those that create more value than they consume. The beauty of this for all of us is that our savings are then used by firms that make resources more valuable than they were before. Everything is scarce to some degree. As a society – as a planet – we want scarce resources to be used to create more of what humans find valuable; to do the opposite is waste, burning money and needlessly using up resources. And our savings are especially scarce, so we'll want them used to create more value so we can earn a "return" on our money. So savers everywhere use their savings (or "capital") to fund enterprises in order to create greater human value out of them.

---

[39] There are cases where the state will compel banks to lend money to failing businesses. Japan, beginning in the 1980s and, more recently, China, are examples. This is bad economics because the supply of scarce savings is diverted from successful firms and because these successful firms must compete with failing state-supported companies that can charge less than it costs to make things and still stay in business. Charles Wheelan, *Naked Money: A Revealing Look at What It Is and Why It Matters* (New York: W.W. Norton, 2016) at 217. In these cases, the state has shackled the Invisible Hand.

Lastly, this almost automatic flow of money – from endeavors that waste resources and toward endeavors that transform resources into something more valuable – is the magic of capitalism. We don't ask state boards or Fearless Leaders to decide where our savings should go; they will automatically flow – through the decisions of millions of individual savers – to make the world more valuable to humans.

Consider an especially illuminating example. One economist performed a study of the economy of the former Soviet Union, measuring, at their true market value all the inputs they used– iron ore, coal, etc. And he also measured at their market value what came out the other end – cars, bed frames, everything people and firms buy – and came to the startling conclusion that the resources consumed by production in the Soviet Union made things <u>worth less than if they'd never been touched at all</u>! They subtracted value. They would have been better off if they left all the iron ore in the ground and sold it to someone who could make good use of it rather than make Soviet cars and other goods.[40] Selling what is below their feet appears to be the one thing at which post-Soviet Russia excels. Over half of their economy is based on pulling oil and gas out of the ground and selling it to someone else who has a good use for it.[41]

Perhaps we shouldn't laugh at the Soviets, though it is important to remember them as a "teachable moment" for those who still fan the dying embers of socialist dreams. That isn't to say that capitalism is immune to stupidity: the dot.com binge in the late 1990s in the US also destroyed over a trillion dollars in value[42] as firms followed the mantra "GBQ," or "Get Big Quick" and were willing to gamble investors' money to buy up Customers, losing money all the way because they were charging less than it cost them to make things. Eventually Mr. Smith's Invisible Hand erased such firms.

---

[40] Ronald I. McKinnon, *The Order of Economic Liberalization* (Baltimore: Johns Hopkins University Press, 1993), Chapter 12.

[41] "Russia's Natural Resources Valued at 60% of GDP," *The Moscow Times*, March 14, 2019, https://www.themoscowtimes.com/2019/03/14/russias-natural-resources-valued-at-60-of-gdp-a64800 (accessed November 30, 2019).

[42] David Kleinbard, "The $1.7 Trillion Dollar Lesson," *CNN*, November 9, 2000, http://www.cnn.com/2000/fyi/news/11/13/dot.com.economics/ (accessed November 30, 2019)

Everybody MUST be a Winner

I apologize for what may have seemed an over-long description of the pure basics of capitalism.

It's a bit protracted because I want to make the case very clear so we can apply the same logic to the company's Customers, Employees, and Owners; they are all acting – in the same way as a company – to produce their own profit.

Anyone reading this is a profit-maximizer. Profit, to be clear, can be found in whatever you find valuable, which isn't always money. I stopped working when I had the chance so I could spend time with my children while they were growing up. I came out way ahead on that trade.

Naturally, we believe that Owners will expect more back from the company than they gave it. If you spend $1000 to buy a share of stock, you expect to make more than $1000 by doing so; otherwise, you'd leave the money in your mattress, where at least no one could waste it on spending that destroys value. Shareholders are profit-maximizers.

But the same is true of Customers and Employees! They won't buy your stuff or work for you unless they get more out of the exchange than they put in to it. And they will hunt carefully for the thing they could buy or the job they could do that gives them the most in excess of what they put in. As we'll see in the next section on "Justice," what Customers and Employees expect is <u>reciprocated</u> profit – they expect that they <u>and</u> the company will profit from the exchange or there won't be more exchanges in the future. Thus, it is a misnomer to say that they are profit-maximizers if by that we mean that they insist on extracting every cent of profit from an exchange of their money or labor.

This idea – that both parties must profit from an exchange – is most commonly covered in economics in discussing the exchange between a company and a Customer. I'll discuss the exchange between a company and its Employees later, but the concepts are the same as for company-Customer exchanges.

One premise: when a company makes something, it needs to sell it for more than it costs to make it; that much is obvious. But the company must <u>make it more valuable than the price it charges</u> or no one will buy it. The Customer will also demand value – profit – in excess of the price. Every time you buy something – unless you are uninformed or being charitable or the seller has deceived you – you will not make the purchase unless you value the thing purchased more than you value what you paid for it. That difference between what you paid and what the purchase is worth to you is called "consumer surplus" in economics. It is the same as profit, except that the Customer rather than the company is keeping it.

So, let's say a new car would be worth $11,000 to me in transportation, convenience, and maybe even in how it looks. If I value having the car at $11,000, and buy it for $10,000, I have made $1000 profit on the sale. If it cost the car company $9000 to make it, then the car company makes $1000 in profit on the sale, too. The car is worth $2000 more than the $9000 it cost to make it. The company and I have split the profit with the $10,000 sale.

The key point here is that <u>the company *must* share</u> some of the value of the car with the Customer. <u>If not, no sale</u>. And <u>the Customer must share</u> some of the value with the company! <u>If not, no cars</u> get made. Both must profit. No free exchange[43] takes place unless both <u>buyer and seller</u> leave the exchange <u>with more than they contributed</u>.

The same principle that Customers and companies will only exchange their money – or their time – if they get more than they give – applies to the Employees of a firm. Employees will trade their time for pay, purpose, and benefits at work, and they will only do so if what they receive is more valuable than their time, creating Employee surplus. Done properly – obeying the rules of reciprocity as I will soon describe – they will contribute more surplus if they know that they will receive surplus in return. And the reverse is true here, too: the company will not hire an Employee unless the Employee creates more value than they cost. If the Employee doesn't earn "Employee surplus," they won't take the job. If the Employee doesn't create surplus for the firm, no job is offered.

And, last, but by no means least, Owners give the firm their savings because they expect profits greater than they could have made elsewhere. And the firm accepts the rate Owners require because the firm can make

---

[43] As with the term "ideal capitalism," I have here used the words "free exchange" to pass over a number of exceptions. Trades made where the company is lying are fraudulent and illegal. Another exception is for monopolies that don't have to share very much with customers because customers have nowhere else to go. (This explains why so many socialist state-owned companies fail to create much value.) And so on. But these exceptions do not undermine the rule. I'll say more about exceptions in the labor market when we get there.

more with the Owners' savings than it costs to pay them. So a company may take your $1000 that pays you 5% per year because the company believes it can make more than 5% per year with it. Whatever they make over 5% is the company's surplus. And you are presumably very happy to earn 5% surplus because there are no better options. (Assuming you have no better options at that same level of risk.)

JUSTICE

Seriously? Profit-Seekers Demand Justice?

My first premise in debunking shareholder primacy, established above, is that Customers, Employees, and Owners are all profit-seekers. Now, let's couple that with the next step.

My second premise is this: Profit-seeking exchanges must obey the rule of reciprocity. The party not reciprocating will be denied profitable trades in the future.

Adam Smith's counter-intuitive triumph was to show that the often selfish human desire to acquire wealth produced tremendous social benefits by creating greater value for us all out of society's available resources. Without this motive, economies fail.

There is another deep human motive without which economies also fail. It is at work in economic exchanges and is overlooked by standard business thinking and our view of companies: Reciprocity.

Reciprocity is the simple rule that I will do things for you if you do things for me. It is the absolute precondition of cooperative social exchanges, and is, for all practical purposes, in our DNA. Our closest primate relatives, chimpanzees, behave reciprocally in food sharing; they share with those who share with them and not with those who don't. "That the close neighbors of our evolutionary ancestors behave reciprocally suggests that this behavior has deep evolutionary roots."[44] The great

---

[44] Ernest Fehr and Simon Gachter, "Reciprocity and Economics: The Economic Implications of *Homo Reciprocans*," *European Economic Review* (Amsterdam: Elsevier Science, 1998), 846. *See also* Elizabeth Hoffman, Kevin McCabe, and Vernon Smith, Behavioral Foundations of Reciprocity: Experimental Economics and Evolutionary Biology, *Economic Inquiry* (Fountain Valley, CA: Western Economic Association International, July 1998) ("[R]esearch in evolutionary psychology (Cosmides and Tooby, 1987, 1989, 1992) suggests that

anthropologist Richard Leakey observed: "We are human because our ancestors learned to share their food and skills in an honored network of obligation."[45]

The transcendent importance of the human sense of reciprocity is evident to researchers as one of the necessary conditions of civilization.[46] Sociologist Robert Cialdini summarizes the evidence amassed by sociologists and anthropologists: "One of the most widespread and basic norms of human culture is embodied in the rule for reciprocation . . . . Consequently, all members of the society are trained from childhood to abide by the rule or suffer serious social disapproval."[47] The late James Q. Wilson of Harvard concluded: "The norm of reciprocity is universal. Virtually everyone who has looked has found it in every culture for which we have the necessary information."[48]

> **The transcendent importance of the human sense of reciprocity is evident to researchers as one of the necessary conditions of civilization.**

---

humans may be evolutionarily predisposed to engage in social exchange using mental algorithms that identify and punish cheaters.").

[45] Richard Leakey and Roger Lewin, *The People of the Lake*, (Glasgow: Avon Books, 1978), 139.

[46] "[R]eciprocity is the vital principle of society." Leonard Hobhouse, *Morals in Evolution: A Study in Comparative Ethics (Classic Reprint)* (London: Forgotten Books, 2017), 12. The "principle of reciprocity . . . is almost a primordial imperative which pervades every relation of primitive life and is the basis on which the entire social and ethical life of primitive civilizations presumably rests." Richard Thurnwald, "Economics in Primitive Communities," *The Annals of the American Academy of Political and Social Science*, 1 (March 1934), 191-192. One scholar finds reciprocity so fundamental to human nature that humans might be redefined as *Homo reciprocus*. Howard Becker, *Man in Reciprocity: Introductory Lectures on Culture, Society and Personality* (Santa Barbara, CA: Greenwood Publishing, 1973), 1.

[47] Robert P. Cialdini, *Influence: The Psychology of Persuasion* (New York: HarperCollins, 2007), 49.

[48] James Q. Wilson, *The Moral Sense* (New York: Free Press, 1997), 65.

In tapping the rule of reciprocity, we harness one of the most powerful human forces to ensure the success of all parties. Ignoring the rules of reciprocity reduces value and can lead firms to ruin. Properly understood by the actors in it, a free economy has a deep commitment to justice in exchanges. It not only takes money away from money-losing enterprises; it takes resources away from swindlers, grifters, and companies wedded to shareholder primacy.

Let me be emphatic: the most productive markets and companies demand the justice of reciprocity. Let's see this in operation in the laboratory and in the marketplace.

Research consistently demonstrates that the most successful strategy in dealing with the reciprocal obligations of others is "tit for tat," that is, to treat the other as the other treats you. If the other treats you badly, do the same in return and their behavior may improve. If the other treats you well, encourage this by reciprocating.[49] And the rule for a business is to begin the cycle of reciprocal generosity by delivering surplus to its Customers, Employees, and Owners unless and until they cease to reciprocate.

---

[49] Robert Axelrod, *The Evolution of Cooperation* (New York: Basic Books, 2006), 27-54. "I never hoped to find wisdom or hope for the future of our species in a computer game, but here it is, in Axelrod's book. Read it." Lewis Thomas, Former Dean of Yale Medical School, back cover review.

Customers and Justice

How does the "loop" of reciprocity work for Customers? The company confers a lot of consumer surplus on their Customers by selling them goods and services that are worth more to the Customer than the Customer pays, creating profit for the Customer. Customers reciprocate by buying more of what the firm is selling thereby creating more surplus – profit – for the firm. Let's be clear that Customers are not being "nice guys" with their loyalty; Customers want to maximize their surplus. If a Customer profits significantly from an exchange, they will want to do it more often.

Customers may also create surplus for the firm by sharing information with it, for example, by responding to surveys on how the company can improve, issues they have had with their purchase, and so forth. Customers who like a company will open and answer surveys and may give favorable reviews – they may well want the company to succeed.

The evidence that these reciprocal loops are powerful has been abundantly clear for decades.

A proxy for consumer surplus is Customer satisfaction. If Customers are extremely satisfied with a company, it means they are receiving lots of consumer surplus when they do business with the firm. So they want to do more business with it more often, as the following evidence will show.

It is not a leap to say that Customer satisfaction is closely linked to Consumer surplus; surplus is the cause, satisfaction the effect. The dramatic differences in buying behavior should erase doubt about the power of this relationship.

Moreover, the finding that highly satisfied customers will do more business with a firm is <u>not</u> news. As long ago as 1991, Xerox found in a survey of 480,000 Customers that "totally satisfied" Customers were <u>six times</u> more likely to repurchase Xerox products in the next 18 months than its merely "satisfied" Customers.[50] The firm I founded, The Great Courses, discovered in the 1990s that Customers who rated their satisfaction with the Company a "9" or "10" on a ten-point scale spent nearly twice as much in the coming year as those who gave us only a "7" or an "8." Extreme satisfaction led to extreme purchasing. A study of financial services found an even more dramatic effect. Clients who rated themselves "very satisfied" gave 16 times more assets to their financial advisors than those who were merely "satisfied."[51]

Given the data above, high Customer satisfaction clearly has a powerful effect on revenue. And this can create great surplus for the company. Consider the effect on several business metrics. Research by Sasser and Reichheld in 1990 across a range of industries reported that creating value for Customers made them more likely to do business with a company and that "a 5% decrease in Customer defections can increase profits by 25% to 85%."[52] A study of banks in Scandinavia reports: "Customer satisfaction . . . has a significant positive effect on all the indicators of Financial Performance . . . . A 1%-point growth increase in Customer Satisfaction gives a 4.9%-point growth in operating income, a 5.6%- point increase in the profit margin (depending on the specification), 6.4-6.8% points in ROA (depending on specification), and 6.8% points in ROE growth."[53]

Perhaps the most-treasured business metric for Owners is the price of the shares they own in a company. The relationship between Customer satisfaction and dramatic improvements in the performance of stock prices – known at least since the Kotter and Heskett study reported in 1992 – remains strong. A report in the *London School of Economics Business Review* in 2017 finds that "when comparing a portfolio chosen based on the American Customer Satisfaction Index (ACSI) versus the

---

[50] James L. Heskett, *et al.*, "Putting the Service-Profit Chain to Work," *Harvard Business Review* (March-April 1994), 165-166.

[51] David Leo and Craig Cmiel, *The Financial Advisor's Success Manual* (New York: AMACOM, 2017), 66.

[52] Frederick F. Reichheld and W. Earl Sasser, Jr., "Zero Defections: Quality Comes to Services," *Harvard Business Review* (September-October 1990), 108.

[53] Jan Eklof, Olga Podkorytova and Aleksandra Malova, "Linking customer satisfaction with financial performance: an empirical study of Scandinavian banks," *Total Quality Management & Business Excellence* 29 (August 2018).

market as a whole, "the results show a 518 per cent growth [in stock price] over the 15 years, compared to only a 31 per cent increase for the S&P 500."[54]

That's an increase 16 times greater than the market at large. And the secret power of Customer satisfaction has been out of the bag for at least the 27 years since Kotter & Heskett. It's been 25 years – a quarter century – since Collins' and Porras' findings. And their book, *Built to Last,* was on the *Business Week* Business Best-Seller list for nearly five years. It's not like the light was hidden under a bushel. And yet, <u>companies remain terrible at this</u>. Frederick Reichheld reports that <u>most</u> companies only have 10-20% more Customers who would recommend them than Customers who would recommend <u>against</u> doing business with the company.[55]

It is an unpardonable act of business malpractice that company leaders have failed to take action on this data, which has been in plain sight for a generation. And yet, the authors of the LSE Business Review study cited above – experts in the measurement of Customer satisfaction and its impact – report that "many companies, even large, high profile companies, don't even know what their Customers think about them and why."[56]

---

[54] Claes Fornell, Forrest Morgeson and Tomas Hult, "Companies that do better by their customers also do better in the stock market," *LSE Business Review* (February 2017). *See also,* Christopher W. Hart, "Beating the Market with Customer Satisfaction," *Harvard Business Review* (March 2007).

[55] Reichheld and Markey, *The Ultimate Question 2.0,* 42.

[56] Fornell, Morgeson, and Hult add: "Without a doubt, many companies seem to either give short-shrift or disregard entirely the importance of customer relationship. The explanation for this is likely to be found in inadequate customer data collection and/or a general misunderstanding of just how valuable satisfied customers are to the firm. . . . Lots of data collection vehicles exist and even lots of satisfaction data exist for many companies. Yet, it is safe to say that there has not been corresponding progress in strategically developing and implementing satisfaction initiatives in many companies."

A methodological aside: There is, as always, some dispute about the best measures to use. Simply asking customers how satisfied they are by itself is surely not as stable as asking a set of questions that look to the same outcome. And <u>all measures must demonstrate power in predicting customer behavior</u>. Surveys can generally be improved by

A Note About the Pains and Joys of Self-Awareness

I am addressing this question to company managers and leaders: Your Customers and Employees all know what they think of your company and the surplus they receive – shouldn't you?

I hope not to wander too far astray from the core of my argument, but allow me five short paragraphs on studying what other people think of you.

In trying to quantify how satisfied Customers are with your company, I share some of the suspicion of "qualitative research" — focus groups or one-on-one interviews. Sample sizes are statistically pointless, and the reports by interviewers can be subjectively filtered.

My suspicions aside, the hard truth about "soft" data is that without a clear understanding of how individual Customers and Employees actually think and talk about their relationship with a firm, quantitative

---

adding questions such as "How strongly do you agree/disagree that the product was worth what you paid?," and "How likely is it that you would recommend our company/product/service to a friend or colleague?" The latter is the question that informs the Net Promoter Score ("NPS") advocated by Frederick Reichheld, a giant in this field. Frederick Reichheld, *The Loyalty Effect: the Hidden Force Behind Growth, Profits, and Lasting Value* (Boston: Harvard Business School Press, 1996); Frederick Reichheld, *Loyalty Rules!: How Today's Leaders Build Lasting Relationships* (Boston: Harvard Business School Press, 2003); Frederick F. Reichheld and Rob Markey, *The Ultimate Question 2.0 (Revised and Expanded Edition): How Net Promoter Companies Thrive in a Customer-Driven World* (Boston: Harvard Business School Press, 2011). There is some dispute about the validity of the NPS by itself. But the insight Reichheld uncovered in subtracting the percentage of customers who are strongly <u>unlikely</u> to recommend a company's product/service from those highly likely to recommend is itself powerful. <u>Most</u> companies are <u>not much above dead even</u>. I add here that it is also possible to "game" or just plain cheat on customer satisfaction measurements, as is the case with almost any business metric. An annual third-party survey to verify internal results should deter gaming.

data is considerably less helpful, in no small part because over-reliance on hard data allows managers to continue to think about Customers as abstractions. There is no "market" – there are people with whom you make exchanges, and understanding the people you serve is the necessary precondition to serving them better.

Aristotle cautioned that we should only expect precision to the extent that the subject at hand admits of it, and to seek no more precision than the subject at hand will admit. If we demanded mathematical precision from all fields of knowledge having to do with humans or even biology, we would never make any progress at all. "We know at a common-sense level that you're never going to have the 'A squared plus B squared equals C squared' when it comes to phenomena of that sort."[57] Mathematics is very precise, but can't tell us a thing about our values or purposes in life. Literary fiction is unabashedly imprecise – it is fictitious! – and yet it can be powerfully informing about some of our deepest questions. I suggest that the search for the right things to do to create value for Customers and Employees begins with some very imprecise but deeply informing inquiries as a prelude to data-gathering.

For your Customers, get up close and invisible. Become the fly on the wall when people talk about your firm. Don't just read survey summaries. Don't say that you know what Customers think because you've read comments, or even if you've listened to some phone calls. I urge anyone who manages or works in a firm or function to sit on the other side of a one-way mirror and watch a focus group – or three or four – about the products or services delivered by your company or group. Without the participants knowing for sure who is listening and watching, let the Customers speak directly about what they think of what you do for a living.

Trust me on this: the experience will make your work life far more tangible to you and, for many, may be a cold splash in the face about things that seemed trivial or merely the concern of your overly-sensitive and unbusiness-like Customer service staff. Been there. Felt that. The experience can be humbling, but it will give the survey results you read a more human and powerful voice. And, yes, your heart may soar when a Customer who loves what you do speaks out. It's an experience you'll want to multiply.

---

[57] Daniel Robinson, "Aristotle on the Knowable," *The Great Ideas of Philosophy,* Part II, Lecture 12, (Chantilly, Virginia: The Teaching Company, 1997), 31

Employees and Justice

The "loop" of reciprocity for Employees is that Employees exchange their time and ingenuity in exchange for pay, tenure, fulfillment from their work, and other benefits. Employee surplus is also exhibited by high satisfaction ratings. And such Employees make a firm much more valuable. This is not new either. In Professor Pfeffer's 1994 classic *Competitive Advantage Through People*, his headline finding was that the five firms that produced the strongest shareholder returns over 20 years did so by managing their workforces better than any rival, equipping them to succeed to a spectacular degree competing in brutal, low-entry cost, low-profit industries. Their returns were all 15,000% or better.[58]

What creates the exceptional performance of firms that manage their Employees well? A ten-year study of over 110,000 Employee surveys reveals that organizations with the most engaged employees achieve:

- 26% less employee turnover
- 100% more unsolicited employment applications
- 20% less absenteeism
- 15% greater employee productivity
- up to 30% greater Customer satisfaction levels
- 65% greater share-price increase[59]

---

[58] The top five stocks, and their percentage returns, were (in reverse order): Plenum Publishing (with a return of 15,689%), Circuit City (a video and appliance retailer; 16,410%), Tyson Foods (a poultry producer; 18,118%), Wal-Mart (a discount chain; 19,807%), and Southwest Airlines (21,775%). Jeffrey Pfeffer, *Competitive Advantage Through People: Unleashing the Power of the Workforce* (Cambridge: Harvard Business School Press, 1994), at 4.

[59] Emma Seppälä and Kim Cameron, "Proof That Positive Work Cultures Are More Productive," Harvard Business Review (December 2015), https://hbr.org/2015/12/proof-that-positive-work-cultures-are-more-productive (accessed August 2, 2019).

Fortune Magazine's annual report, "The 100 Best Places to Work" found in 2016 that Employees at these top 100 firms were 13 times more likely to express a commitment to stay with their employers for a long time. How does that affect the bottom line? Companies, on average, spend 12% of their operating budgets on the costs of Employee turnover, which runs anywhere between 90% and 200% of an Employee's wages. At the 100 Best Places to Work, that cost is half that – saving 6% of a company's operating budget each year.[60] A good profit is in the 10% range. Adding another 6% of a company's cash to the bottom line would increase those profits by 60%.

And, as with Customer satisfaction's effect on stock values, and as with Kotter and Heskett's findings decades ago, high Employee satisfaction produces greater wealth for the Owners of such firms. Finance Professor Alex Edmans summarizes his research: "28 years of data found that firms with high Employee satisfaction outperform their peers by 2.3% to 3.8% *per year* in long-run stock returns – 89% to 184% cumulative – even after controlling for other factors that drive returns. Moreover, the results suggest that it's Employee satisfaction that causes good performance, rather than good performance allowing a firm to invest in Employee satisfaction."[61]

The online company rating service for Employees, Glassdoor.com, examined the stock effects of high rankings for the *Fortune* best places to work and Glassdoor's own list generated through voluntary ratings online. Between 2009 and 2014, a portfolio of *Fortune*'s "Best Companies to Work For" companies outperformed the S&P 500 by 84.2 percent, while a similar portfolio of Glassdoor's "Best Places to Work" outperformed the overall market by 115.6 percent.[62]

---

[60] "Connecting People and Purpose: 7 Ways High-Trust Organizations Retain Talent," *Great Place to Work*, http://learn.greatplacetowork.com/rs/520-AOO-982/images/GPTW-Fortune-100Best-Report-2016.pdf (accessed November 30, 2019).

[61] Alex Edmans, "28 Years of Stock Market Data Shows a Link Between Employee Satisfaction and Long-Term Value," *Harvard Business Review* (March 2016).

[62] Andrew Chamberlain, "Does Company Culture Pay Off? Analyzing Stock Performance of 'Best Places to Work' Companies," *Glassdoor* (March 2015). Chamberlain's study compares the effect of three different portfolio strategies for buying and holding "Best Company" stocks, each of which produces exceptional gains.

"High engagement" and "extremely satisfied" Employees are in the same position as extremely satisfied Customers – they are receiving value from the firm in excess of what they contribute to the firm. But your co-workers aren't buying a product, so how can you create "surplus" for them?

Doing it Less and Enjoying it More – Bossing Autonomous Beings

Again, I ask for your patience, as I personalize the search for Employee satisfaction.

I hunted for years with surveys, meetings, and consultants to find how best to raise Employee satisfaction. Then I found Gallup's 1999 book, "First, Break All The Rules," in which they described the 12-question instrument they had created over the course of two million Employee surveys.[63] They had built the survey so that the questions were those most linked with the success of the business. I went through this book like I was speed-shopping at a supermarket. Moreover, bigger paychecks were not – as many employers fear – the key to success.

Fear this instead. Something far more difficult than giving everyone a raise is required. A change in the structure of work and in the human relations between management and Employee is often central to success. Let me broaden the assertion I made that there are no "markets," there are people with whom you make exchanges. Similarly, companies are a legal abstraction; people are real.

As Gallup explains it, the most important question is the first: "At work, I know what is expected of me." If you fail on this first question, none of the other 11 questions really matter. This was a surprise to me. But then I thought about what <u>not</u> knowing what was expected of you at work would be like. Lack of clarity about the job leaves Employees in a fog; some days they come to work and are showered with pennies from heaven while other days they get whacked across the back of the head – and they can't be sure why either happened! Almost certainly, someone in charge hasn't

---

[63] Marcus Buckingham and Curt Coffman, *First, Break All the Rules: What the World's Greatest Managers Do Differently* (New York: Simon & Schuster, 1999).

made up his or her mind on who should do what by when <u>and why and explained it</u>. This is the fault of the "organizing class" of Employees, from supervisors to the C-suite. Job One is to get clear on what needs to be done and why, who needs to do it, and on what schedule.

I won't detail here all of the steps in Gallup's process or that of the Hay Group, Towers-Perrin, Medallia or others who lead in research in this field. What I want to underscore, as a recovering autocrat, is that as leaders and managers of other people we are obliged to create clarity, to listen carefully, and to explain regularly what we want and <u>why</u> we want it to other <u>autonomous human beings</u>. This cost me something in time and humility – and it was all worthwhile.

Owners and Justice

I don't mean to belittle providing justice to Owners with a short section on the loop of reciprocity for them. As I argue, the elevation of Customers and Employees should not lead to the demotion of Owners, particularly given that, without capital, no new business can get started.

Only brief comment is needed because the loop of reciprocity for Owners is most easily understood and measured because, in recent decades, the interests of shareholders have triumphed. They give their savings to the firm now and the firm produces a profit in the future with the money.

We ordinarily think of Owners as dispassionate calculators of returns. But then there are the Berkshire Hathaway annual meetings which more nearly resemble rock concerts than academic conferences.[64] Owners not only enjoy making money by investing; they may also take pleasure in identifying with great companies. It's the same as rooting for your local football team and wearing their jersey – except that it pays.

It is clear that Customers, Employees, and Owners respond positively to companies that share surplus with them. They are driven by their own profit-seeking and the power of reciprocity.

---

[64] Much must be added about investments that favor "Environmental, Social, and Governmental" scorecards ("ESG"), as well as the related concept of Corporate Social Responsibility ("CSR"). Much will be said later when we address open-ended stakeholder theories under the heading, "What if <u>everyone</u> had a stake?"

VENGEANCE

The Dark Side

What happens to companies that do not share surplus? What happens if you think a company has delivered a product worth barely what you paid? Or less than you paid? What happens to an employer whose C-Suite Employees park their pricey German cars at work but will not increase Employee bonuses or pay when the firm is generating big profits?

Let's take a look at the Dark Side of The Force of Reciprocity.

The Bitter Taste of Peppercorns

Assume that you are a "shareholders only" partisan and therefore believe that the purpose of the company is to create profits for the Owners. A corollary that follows is that when a firm engages in an exchange with Customers or Employees, the firm should capture as much of the value in that transaction as possible, so that the wealth of the firm's Owners is maximized.

In the car example earlier, where the car costs $9,000 to make and I value the car at $11,000, the car manufacturer would maximize its profits by charging me $10,999 for it. (If they charge $11,000, I have no reason to trade my money for their car; the money is worth the same to me in my pocket.) In my earlier example where the company and I split the $2000 difference between the $9000 it cost to make the car and the $11,000 it is worth to me, the company has sacrificed $999 in profit. So, to a "shareholders-first-and-only" firm, they should charge as much as they can and still get me to buy the car.

And the same for wages; a company should offer me a dollar more than is needed to have me turn down other offers and work for them. It will be a close call, but I'll take the job.

So, the profit-maximizing course of action is to charge Customers a price just below that where they wouldn't buy from you and to pay Employees barely more than the amount where they would stop working for you. An economist friend digested whole chapters of microeconomics texts this way: "Economic theory says firms should give workers a utility package equal to their best alternative plus a tiny increment. Similar for customers. Not really sharing." Please note that this maxim is mathematically derived and theoretical – I reject it based on empirical evidence taken from the real world.

What should be added, by extension, is that investors should only get a dollar more than they need to keep their savings invested in the firm. Any payment greater than that amount does not maximize the profits of the firm. As long as the firm still gets the transaction – a sale, a day's work, more capital – paying a dollar more than that amount is a waste of profits. The shareholder primacy argument would say, of course, that all those profits are being amassed by the firm so they can be distributed to the Owners eventually.

In the law, the minimum amount recognized as material in an exchange is a "peppercorn,"[65] and I shall refer to this argument as the "Peppercorn Rule:" never pay a peppercorn more than is needed to gain the transaction. This has some strong intuitive appeal in part because it seems simple, especially if it is coupled with the usual supply and demand curves that set a proper price point we have seen since our first economics course. But how can the peppercorn rule be correct in light of the evidence of massive increases in profits for those firms that share bushels of surplus with their Customers? Or in light of the evidence of startling increases in value for firms that offer far more than a peppercorn in extra surplus for their Employees?

The principal failings of the peppercorn theory are that 1) it considers only how one party in a two-party exchange will act to maximize their surplus and 2) it gives insufficient weight to the value of reciprocity or the converse risk of vengeance.

Recall the earlier proof that a company's Customers and Employees are also profit-maximizers. Just as the firm seeks to maximize surplus, Customers, Employees, and Owners also seek to maximize their surplus. Now add the Rule of Reciprocity, under which Customers, Employees, and Owners take strong action to reciprocate the way they are treated. This presents great dangers to a peppercorn firm and great opportunities for a reciprocally generous one. Consider first the evidence from the field of behavioral economics and, second, the findings about the power of reciprocity in real-world exchanges with Customers and Employees.

---

[65] "Consideration may be as small as a peppercorn, if that is what the offeror is bargaining to receive in exchange for his or her promise." Frey and Frey, *Contract Law* (Boston: Cengage, 2001), 44. The Masonic Lodge of St. George's, Bermuda, rents the Old State House as its lodge for the annual sum of a single peppercorn, presented to the Governor of Bermuda on a velvet cushion atop a silver platter, in an annual ceremony performed since 1816 on or about 23 April. "Peppercorn ceremony draws Freemasons from US, UK and Canada." *The Royal Gazette* (22 April 2013). (accessed November 30, 2019).

Partners and Peppercorns: Vengeance in the Laboratory

We've reviewed the surprisingly large returns to Owners if surplus is created for the key partners of a company in value-creation.

What happens if you short-change your partners by sharing as little as possible? Customers, Employees, and Owners who think you left too little on the table for them can and will react strongly. People don't just reciprocate bad offers with bad offers – they <u>retaliate</u> against players who share too little, even at a cost to themselves, an instinct evident in childhood.[66]

Consider experiments with the game "Ultimatum." In Ultimatum, one player is given a sum of money, some of which they must share with another player. If the second player rejects the offered share, neither player gets anything. Economic theory tells us that the second player should be willing to accept any offer – even a peppercorn – since that is more than they will receive if they reject the offer. But that's not how humans behave; we actively punish the peppercorn players. "In the Ultimatum Game, the game-theoretic equilibrium – the proposer offers a penny and the responder takes it – almost never happens in real life. Proposers tend to offer about 40% of the pot, and responders frequently reject offers of less than 20% to 30%."[67] In one experiment, if participants were informed that another player had made a stingy offer to an earlier player, <u>three quarters</u> of the participants were willing to receive less so they could share it with fair players rather than receive more that they could share with stingy players.

Ultimatum's results are no surprise if we understand that the rule of reciprocity is essential for society to succeed. All of us instinctively punish rule-breakers in order to deter anti-social behaviors and to promote the success of mutually beneficial exchanges. Again, from Professor Cialdini's summary of the data: "For the most part, there is a

---

[66] The great childhood psychologist Jean Piaget observed that ". . . reciprocity stands so high in the eyes of the child that he will apply it even where to us it seems to border on crude vengeance." Jean Piaget, *The Moral Judgment of the Child* (New York: Simon and Schuster, 1997), 217.

[67] Scott P. Stevens, *Games People Play: Game Theory in Life, Business, and Beyond* (Chantilly, Virginia: The Teaching Company, 2008), 56.

genuine distaste for an individual who fails to conform to the dictates of the reciprocity rule."[68]

This is worrisome data from the psychology laboratories for peppercorn firms. More worrisome is how this works in the real world to benefit a peppercorn firm's rivals.

Customer Vengeance in the Marketplace

The data show that leaving little surplus for Customers leaves them with very little incentive to buy a second time. Recall that at The Great Courses, we found that even a drop from 9-10 on a ten point scale to 7-8 on the same scale can cut downstream spending as much as 50%. Or worse – Xerox found that a 4 on a five-point scale cut downstream spending to only 17% of what it would be if Customers gave a "5" on the same scale.

Here is a vital mystery: where does all that lost downstream spending go?

Much of it is probably going to your competitors. AT&T's research in the 1980s found that Customers who rated their satisfaction with AT&T a 5 on a 5-scale were only 10% likely to migrate to a competitor; those who rated AT&T a 4 on a 5-scale were 40% likely to migrate.[69] To restate: one notch from extremely satisfied to merely satisfied increased the odds of giving a Customer to a competitor by 400%.

A company that is not sharing surplus with Customers is in the business of sharing Customers with competitors. There is a standard business metric that reveals the impact of Customer migration – Market Share, the percentage of Customers in the market for a particular product or service who buy from each firm competing in that market. Here's the prediction: if Customers believe they get more value from an exchange with a company than from a competitor, they will migrate to the better value firm, and that firm will get larger; it will grow.

---

[68] Cialdini, *Influence*, 34.

[69] Bradley Gale and Robert Wood, *Managing Customer Value* (New York: Free Press, 2010), 78.

A company that is not sharing surplus with Customers is in the business of sharing Customers with competitors.

Here's what just some of the evidence shows in relation to this common-sense proposition. AT&T researchers found one question in a group of Customer satisfaction questions – "Was the product worth what you paid for it?" – almost perfectly predictive of changes in market share within four months.[70] The Profit Impact of Market Strategies (PIMS) database of 3,000 businesses collects detailed information on finances, advertising, perceived quality, Customer satisfaction and other variables. In 1996, this data revealed that improving quality compared to competitors increased market share by 4% *per year* (so that in 10 years such a firm would be roughly 150% its original size).

It was true then, and it is true now, that delivering value to Customers will draw them toward a value-sharing firm. Frederick Reichheld reported on some results of the satisfaction metric he favors, the Net Promoter Score (NPS) – subtracting Customers who are highly unlikely to recommend your product/service from those who are likely to do so. If 80% of your Customers are likely to recommend you, but 10% are unlikely to do so, your NPS is 70%. Great companies such as USAA, Amazon, and Costco, have NPS of 60 to 80%. The impact: "NPS leaders tend to grow at more than twice the rate of their competitors," according to Reichheld.[71] A team of researchers studying the US health care arm of Philips found that relative NPS explained 90% of the changes in market share between Philips and its key competitors.[72] Just to de-code the business abstraction: increasing market share means you have acquired new Customers and/or more spending from your existing Customers.[73]

---

[70] Ibid., 81-82 (citing a 1991 speech by Ray Kordupleski at the American Marketing Association's Customer Satisfaction Congress).

[71] Reichheld and Markey, *The Ultimate Question 2.0*, 42.

[72] Ibid., 64.

[73] The absolute score on almost any customer satisfaction measure is, of course, not wholly relevant except to measure your company against its earlier performance; a score of 50 now is great versus an earlier 30. The real measure of concern is your score against those of other companies in your market; a score of 50 now may not be so good if your rival scores a 70.

Customers who give very low scores, say 3 or less on a 5-point scale, have almost certainly experienced "negative surplus" and may feel cheated by the exchange. You will probably never hear from them again (unless you overhear them trash-talking you on social media) – they are spending all of their money with your competitors. In order to reciprocate, these Customers or Employees retaliate to even the score in tit-for-tat. Partners respond to peppercorn offers with small or no future contributions, and they will respond to a generous offer generously, especially if a peppercorn firm's rival makes it. Thus, if you left a peppercorn for your partners, you have helped to maximize your rival's long-term profits.

Considered in a positive light, we can say that highly satisfied Customers and Employees have stopped shopping – they have taken themselves out of the marketplace, depriving rivals access to the stream of revenue and productivity they can supply. The peppercorn theory misses a critical surplus-creating opportunity: Customers and Employees are a strategic resource. Because they do not migrate, highly satisfied Customers and Employees are, in the parlance of strategy theorists, "sticky." Or, similarly, high satisfaction creates a high "switching cost" for potentially wayward partners. Every sale a CEO firm makes to a highly satisfied Customer not only ensures that the firm's future will be bright; it also denies a rival access to sales now and in the future.

> **Every sale a CEO firm makes to a highly satisfied Customer not only ensures that the firm's future will be bright; it also denies a rival access to sales now and in the future.**

Employee Vengeance in the Workplace

Recall that high Employee satisfaction produces massive gains in the performance of a company – on measures that Owners treasure.

So what becomes of a firm that serves peppercorns to its Employees? How worthy is the view that each increase in Employee pay, for example, is a deadweight loss to a company's profits? That view is dominant among investors. A study in *The American Economic Review* found that announcements of pay increases reduce market valuations dollar-for-dollar, consistent with the zero-sum view that a dollar paid to workers is a dollar taken away from shareholders.[74]

On this theory, by keeping wages at peppercorn levels, we should be maximizing the value of the company. Alex Edmans, Professor of Finance at the London School of Business, quotes one stock analyst who disfavors Costco stock because Costco deliberately pays their Employees more than competitors and makes Employees quickly eligible for health benefits. The analyst says: "[Costco's] management is focused on ... Employees to the detriment of shareholders. To me, why would I want to buy a stock like that?"[75] Since the date of that analyst's complaint in 2003, Costco's stock is up 860% versus 280% for the S&P 500.[76]

As the saying goes, you reap what you sow. In a close comparison to Customer behavior when Customers feel they have been short-changed, a short-changed Employee does just as a short-changed Customer does – they leave. The Great Place to Work company, which, unsurprisingly, conducts the surveys for *Fortune*'s "Great Places to Work," found in an analysis of the 2016 results of that survey that turnover at the best firms was half that of industry peers." Recall the earlier finding from Great Places to Work: The study found that "the average cost of turnover is 90% - 200% of the exiting Employee's base salary, and 12% of a company's operating budget." Six percent of most companies' operating budget could be a very high fraction of their total profits. Price Waterhouse Coopers reports that "[f]or companies at the high end of the spectrum, at the 75th percentile, turnover costs are equivalent to nearly 40% of earnings!"[77]

---

[74] John Abowd, "The Effect of Wage Bargains on the Stock Market Value of the Firm," *The American Economic Review* 79 (1989), 774-800, http://www.jstor.org/stable/1827932, (accessed July 31, 2019).

[75] "A Showdown at the Checkout for Costco," *Bloomberg Business*, August 28, 2003, https://www.bloomberg.com/news/articles/2003-08-27/a-showdown-at-the-checkout-for-costco (accessed November 30, 2019).

[76] In addition to other stellar officers, the second wise man of Berkshire Hathaway, Charles Munger, is on Costco's Board of Directors. Maybe he knows something that our failed analyst does not.

[77] (emphasis in original). "Driving the bottom line: improving retention," *Saratoga Human Resources Service*, 2006, https://www.shrm.org/hr-today/news/hr-magazine/Documents/saratoga-improving-retention.pdf (accessed November 30, 2019).

And which Employees are most likely to leave a peppercorn firm? The best ones, of course! Those with high skills and productivity are sending their resumes to and getting good job offers from a peppercorn firm's competitors. Recall that companies with high Employee satisfaction receive twice as many job applications. A weak firm effectively cuts its share of the potential Employee market in half. And the Employees that a peppercorn firm sheds may often go to work for competitors. By treating Employees as a mere cost, a company acts as a training ground and recruiting service for other firms, including its more successful rivals.

> **By treating Employees as a mere cost, a company acts as a training ground and recruiting service for other firms, including its more successful rivals.**

Beyond turnover, here's what the data suggest about sowing peppercorns for Employees, expressed in some standard business metrics followed most closely by investors: "In studies by the Queen's School of Business and by the Gallup Organization . . . . In organizations with low Employee engagement scores, they experienced 18% lower productivity, 16% lower profitability, 37% lower job growth, and 65% lower share price over time."[78]

Let me make two key reservations about Employee satisfaction here which I will emphasize below. One, in accord with the rule of reciprocity, I'm not suggesting that companies exist to create a workers' paradise; simple generosity to workers is a road to ruin unless workers reciprocate.[79]

My second reservation is that I am not claiming that Employees are able to move frictionlessly from job to job in search of the best employer. That search has surely been made simpler by the transparency afforded by Glassdoor.com and similar online ratings. But, no matter how much they know, people may be trapped by circumstances to a specific area, may lack any power to negotiate with employers and therefore have their

---

[78] Seppälä and Cameron, "Proof That Positive Work Cultures Are More Productive," *Harvard Business Review* (December 2015).

[79] The example of Malden Mills' Massachusetts factory is instructive in Jeffrey Harrison and Douglas Bosse, "How much is too much? The limits to generous treatment of stakeholders," *Business Horizons* (2013) 56, 313.

value underrated – and, over time, an Employee may well build up expertise specific to a particular company, limiting their outside marketability, though their value to the company is rising as expertise accumulates.

Nevertheless, as I believe the evidence overwhelmingly shows, a firm that exploits such flaws in the labor market will lose value for its Owners; even if Employees may not be able to withdraw bodily from a firm by leaving, they can and do withdraw their minds – they will not give the extra measure of effort and ingenuity that highly engaged Employees do.[80] It is good news that exploitation is a road to competitive failure. My reasonably educated conclusion is that the history of capitalism is strewn with the hollow remains of companies where Employees treated peppercorn companies as badly as those companies treated them. Tit-for-tat: Gone!

---

[80] "Numerous studies, theoretical and empirical, have argued that positive reciprocity can explain why workers perform even when they have ample opportunity for shirking. [In our survey of 11,453 German households] we show that positively reciprocal inclinations are positively associated with working overtime while the reverse is true for negative reciprocity." Thomas Dorman, Armin Falk, David Huffman, and Uwe Sunde, "Homo Reciprocans: Survey evidence on Behavioural Outcomes," *The Economic Journal* (Royal Economic Society, March 2009), 593.

THE CEO FORMULA

The Obvious Fallacy of Shareholder Supremacy, Customer Supremacy, or Employee Supremacy.

In summary, the evidence shows that creating surplus for Customers greatly improves its results for Owners. The same holds for Employees. But – critically – a sole focus on Owners, or solely on Employees, or solely on Customers, destroys value that could have been shared by all three.

Here, we resolve the paradox with which we began: how is it that by focusing on Owners' returns, a firm drastically reduces Owners' returns? And how is it that a company focused on C <u>and</u> E <u>and</u> O does more than twice as well as one that seeks to maximize results for <u>only</u> Customers and Employees, demoting Owners?

The problem is that sole focus on any of Customers, Employees, and is logically and financially absurd if taken to its maximizing entailment. I repeat the following paragraphs from my introduction.

- Shareholders will do best in the short run if product quality is diluted and salaries are cut, or if productive investments are foregone so the company can buy back its own shares and inflate its share price. This may improve results in the short run, but it will damage a firm's long-term value as Customers and Employees leave and as short-term Owners harvest their profits and go elsewhere, like locusts.

- Customers will prosper in the short run if product quality is vastly enhanced and prices are set near zero. An old Dilbert cartoon quotes Ratbert: "We have new market research to show that Customers want product quality to be greatly increased and everything should be free."

Kotter and Heskett warn about this "Customer is King" scenario in their 1992 study. "[I]n a firm with a strong Customer orientation but without much concern for Employees and stockholders....managers try hard to meet Customers' changing needs, even if that means significantly reducing margins and working Employees very long hours. That strategy works well for a while, but eventually capital becomes too scarce to invest in much needed new products and services. Furthermore, Employees start to feel exploited and stop working hard for the Customer. As a result, such firms find it harder and harder to meet changing Customer requirements."[81]

- Employee as King? Most managers know that a firm run solely for its Employees cannot last because some grifters will exploit it. Pushed to its logical and financial extreme, we could create a happy workplace for Homer Simpson in a La-Z-Boy with a pile of donuts handy, but no investor would park money there and no Customer would buy whatever Homer does or makes, though Homer might be extremely satisfied. Some dot.com era excesses come to mind.

---

[81] Kotter and Heskett, *Corporate Culture and Performance*, 54-55.

The Triumph of CEO

Why is "CEO" the right answer? First, the CEO firm maximizes contributions. In light of the data on Customer and Employee satisfaction, the potential contribution of resources from a firm's Customers and Employees is an enormous source of untapped value for many firms. A firm is logically and financially unimaginable without all three groups. The CEO strategy wins because a firm that receives more contributions from each will have more cash at lower cost from its Owners to invest, more revenue and information from its Customers, and more productive work and innovation from its Employees than a rival.

Consider also "negative contributions." Part of the reason CEO firms create up to seven times as much value as peppercorn firms is that Owner-primacy/peppercorn firms are being vengefully punished in the marketplace and workplace, bleeding Customer revenue and Employee effort. It's much easier to be seven times better than a self-destructive opponent.

> **It's much easier to be seven times better than a self-destructive opponent.**

Second, the CEO firm minimizes wasteful distributions. If C, E, and O are all highly important, no one group enjoys the power to harvest more than its share of value created because it is checked by the need to create value for the other two. There are only three places the money can go – to C, to E, or to O. Thus, a Scrooge Owner, a Ratbert Customer, and a Homer Simpson Employee will produce less surplus in total and especially less for the short-changed groups, making the firm vulnerable to competitors. A business that refuses to subsidize Scrooge, Ratbert, and Homer has more resources available for more fruitful exchanges.[82] Moreover,

---

[82] Let's be clear about the obvious: that C, E, and O are each highly important does not mean that they are to be treated equally at all times – or even most of the time – though they are all regarded as equally important to the firm's long-term success. However, different groups will be able to create more value than others at different times. When a firm is in start-up phase, Owners are likely to be most important

reciprocity is a hard check on distributions that destroy value: no group may receive distributions in excess of the value they would create in exchange for the distribution.

When, from the perspective of all three groups, should the firm share its cumulative surplus with any of them? The firm should share the surplus received from all of the groups with whichever group or groups will create the most new surplus in exchange for the shared value. The trade is reciprocal: create surplus for the firm, and the firm will create surplus for you. The firm could decide to invest heavily in new product development if Customer spending on those new products would produce more new profit than anything the Employees and Owners could do in exchange for the same money. The calculation applies across the triad – Employees might increase productivity and innovation and, therefore, profit – in exchange for profit-sharing; Owners might accept dividend reduction in exchange for new capital equipment that will lead to increased profit, and so on.

The CEO Formula's departure from shareholder primacy is this:

1) A company's purpose is not to maximize profits for its Owners.

2) A company's purpose is to create maximum mutual profit with Customers, Employees, and Owners and to recycle the company's share from those exchanges to do more of the same.

Let me make that statement more concrete. As I'll elaborate in the next section, here is the universal form of the CEO Formula expressed as the purpose of every business:

- Make world-class, insanely great products and services for Customers who will buy repeatedly and profitably;
- Help your Employees build great lives with the work they do and the profits they create through productive and inventive effort; and
- Protect and grow for the long run the savings Owners have entrusted to you.

---

because the firm can't hire employees or create products to sell without some capital from investors. A new invention in product quality may merit the largest allocation of surplus to Customers so the company can get its winning new product to market. Who gets priority at any given time depends on who can create the most surplus in exchange for surplus.

The CEO Formula requires the firm to create as much reciprocated surplus for all three parties, only one portion of whose success – Owners – is measured by financial statements, and even then only weakly. Financial statements must be evaluated alongside measures of

- Customer surplus (measured by satisfaction, Net Promoter, and other proxy scores) coupled with
- profits per Customer and
- Employee surplus (measured by satisfaction, turnover, and other proxies) coupled with
- profits per Employee.

An entire literature has been produced on the ways to change financial statements to make them more useful to managers and to investors. I recognize that my edicts here are very brief. That is by design. There are many technical issues here, covered in detail by experts,[83] so I won't venture more than to say that firms must measure these reciprocal relationships and their future value carefully and scientifically. Having done this at my own company, though, I can say that forecasting the value of relationships with three parties is easier, more obvious, and more useful than GAAP accounting, which is sometimes just plain bizarre.

Corporate Purpose and the "Value Maximization" and Extrusion Nozzle Problems

While one of the long-run effects of the CEO Formula will be to increase the market value of the firm, that is not its purpose. Its purpose is to enrich the firm and the partners who join it in value-creation. No sane

---

[83] *See, e.g.*, Baruch Lev and Feng Gu, *The End of Accounting and the Path Forward for Investors and Managers* (Hoboken, New Jersey: Wiley Finance Series, 2016). An extensive treatment of the measures that would account for Customer and Employee surplus is detailed in Frederick Reichheld, *The Loyalty Effect: The Hidden Force Behind Growth, Profits, and Lasting Value* (Boston: Harvard Business School Press, 1996), Chapter 8.

orator ever called on his people to risk themselves or spend their lives so the firm could "Maximize the net present value of all future cash flows!"

The CEO Formula will, in fact, significantly increase the net present value of future cash flows, but that's a means of keeping score on how much the firm is giving and receiving value, not the game itself. As Professor Jensen has written, "...if we simply tell all participants in an organization that its sole purpose is to maximize value, we will not get maximum value for the organization."[84] For that, a firm needs purpose. Its actions must have meaning. And I repeat again that markets and corporations are abstractions – Customers, Employees, and Owners are *real*. Defining a company's purpose in its human effects is inspiring and it clears away a lot of business buzz-talk that obscures rather than illuminates what we do.

It is no wonder that some companies are so driven. Look at some of the defining goals of extraordinary companies listed by Jim Collins, each of which is devoted to *humans:*[85]

> "To make people happy." Disney

> "To give ordinary folk the chance to buy the same things as rich people." Wal-Mart

> "To preserve and improve human life." Merck

> "To give unlimited opportunity to women." Mary Kay

But what do you do if your company makes extrusion nozzles? Or sewage waste treatment chemicals? How is a company leader supposed to find the rhetoric that summons the best in everyone if that's where you have to begin?

Truly, it isn't that difficult. Every company can and should strive to provide the best possible goods and services to its customers. Every company can and should strive to enrich the lives of its employees. And every company can and should work to produce strong returns for those with whose savings they have been entrusted.

---

[84] Michael Jensen, "Value Maximization, Stakeholder Theory, and the Corporate Objective Function," *Journal of Applied Corporate Finance*, Fall 2001, 16.

[85] James Collins, "21st Century Start-Up," *Inc. Magazine*, October 1997, 46

Consider an especially hard case, a company that crushes rock for a living. Seriously. They quarry rocks and crush them for manufacturing and construction. They are only a step away from a prisoner's worst day – as the song goes, "breaking rocks in the hot sun."

And, yet – and I am not making this up – Graniterock is one of the best companies in America, having won the Malcolm Baldridge National Quality Award in 1992. They were the first California company ever to win it.

What is Graniterock's corporate purpose? "Graniterock thrives when our People thrive. We exist to provide a place where inspired People can do their best work – building great projects, producing quality materials, and developing enduring customer relationships."[86]

I find that pretty inspired, especially because it wipes away the elitist cobwebs that often obscure the dignity of work itself rather than valorizing only its downstream effects.

So, what to do? I repeat the universal form of the CEO Formula:

- Make world-class, insanely great products and services – even extrusion nozzles – for Customers who will buy repeatedly and profitably;
- Help your Employees build great lives with the work they do and the profits they create through productive and inventive effort; and
- Protect and grow for the long run the savings Owners have entrusted to you.

---

[86] Posted by Kevin Jeffery on March 18, 2015, https://www.graniterock.com/blogs/strategic-planning-start-at-the-core.

But Wait! There's More. A Lot More.

The total surplus created by a CEO firm will be greater for all three groups than for an "O" only firm. Because much value is lost by prioritizing Owners above Customers and Employees, then we can also say that the CEO Formula brings us closer to the *summum bonum*, the highest good, of economics – creating as much value as possible with as few resources as possible. And to achieve that, the firm must deliberately create reciprocated surplus with all three of its partners. I believe the evidence makes clear that Owners will be far more satisfied with the longer run results of the CEO formula.

What I have not tried here to quantify is the enormous improvements in the lives of Customers and Employees that would be created if the CEO Formula were more widely understood and adopted. Consider just a few possibilities.

I've already discussed the impact of paying Employees for their increased productivity since the early 1980s: One study concluded that the average Employee would be making another $5000 per year.[87] Another estimated that American wages would be 50% higher than they are today.[88] Let me add this: had pay been explicitly linked to increased productivity, productivity would almost certainly have risen even more.

---

[87] Such increased pay would, of course, raise a great deal of revenue for the state, now taxed more highly as ordinary income rather than capital gains had it been distributed as a "qualified" dividend to shareholders. Google "qualified dividends" if tax intricacies speak to you.

[88] "The Productivity–Pay Gap," Economic Policy Institute, updated August 2018, https://www.epi.org/productivity-pay-gap/ (accessed November 30, 2019).

How about the quality of our lives? We are or have been, almost all of us, Employees. Highly engaged Employees are, unsurprisingly, much more satisfied with their lives than disengaged Employees. I'll supply evidence here, but surely you or someone you know well has had their life flattened by a bad workplace or uplifted by a great one. If you needed proof for what we all take to be obvious because we are humans capable of memory and sympathy, rest assured that it is true everywhere you look. Separate studies among Pakistani army soldiers,[89] Turkish teachers,[90] American agricultural extension agents,[91] and Finnish dentists[92] all find a strong relationship between satisfaction with work life and satisfaction with life. And the causal arrow points from the workplace to life. If just 10% more full-time Employees in the U.S. alone were fully engaged with their work, 13.6 million Americans would lead better, more fulfilled lives. And their companies would prosper.

Here's another perspective on Employees. Employees are trading hours, years, maybe decades of their lives in exchange for their jobs. While most of us treasure the moments we spend with friends and family, it is necessarily the case that we will spend the greatest fraction of the waking

---

[89] Summira Naz, "Relationship of Life Satisfaction and Job Satisfaction among Pakistani Army Soldiers," *Journal of Business Research* 1 (2015): 20, https://pdfs.semanticscholar.org/f038/3e7eb570efbfd334783a34f4ab7c81da0544.pdf, (accessed November 30, 2019).

[90] Belgin Aydintan and Hakan Koc, "The Relationship between Job Satisfaction and Life Satisfaction: An Empirical Study on Teachers," *International Journal of Business and Social Science* 10 (October 2016): 77, https://www.researchgate.net/publication/314261752_The_Relationship_between_Job_Satisfaction_and_Life_Satisfaction_An_Empirical_Study_on_Teachers, (accessed November 30, 2019).

[91] Kansas State University. "Employees Who Are Engaged In Their Work Have Happier Home Life." *ScienceDaily*, August 25, 2009, www.sciencedaily.com/releases/2009/08/090824115911.htm (accessed November 30, 2019).

[92] Jari Hakanen and Wilmar Schaufeli, "Do burnout and work engagement predict depressive symptoms and life satisfaction? A three-wave seven-year prospective study," *Journal of Affective Disorders*, (December 10, 2012), 415-424 https://www.sciencedirect.com/science/article/abs/pii/S0165032712001966.

hours of our adult lives getting to and from work and working. A company that fails to realize and act on the reality that its Employees are literally "spending their lives" at work is both missing an opportunity and is complicit in human tragedy. Firms that fail to create significant reciprocated surplus for their Employees cost us, not just in dollars, but in lost years of better lives for which no real compensation is possible. This isn't lefty rhetoric: It is a stone-cold fact that employers are stewards of people's working lives.

For Customers, "consumer surplus" can and often is measured – though finding people's price points via surveys and other commonly used instruments is fraught. Assuming the data are trustworthy, a firm can calculate the added economic benefit it has conferred on its Customers. The converse – eliminating extreme dissatisfaction – would also be life-enhancing: think about the last experience you had with a snarling, impenetrable Customer service system and what that did to your day – or your life. Insurance companies are becoming a punchline and a presidential campaign issue. Or how about a product that just doesn't work for you and is almost impossible to fix without several calls, e-mails, and a service visit or two?

Again, let me offer the perspective of time spent. For Customers, the relationship between hours of life and spending is obvious with a bit of reflection. If someone gives you $100 for your product, they have exchanged hours spent working at their job for your firm's goods or services. Assume, generously, that your Customer makes $100,000 per year. If taxes consume 35% of that, your Customer earns $65,000 per year in take-home pay. Again, generously assuming that your Customer only has to work 40 hours per week and takes two weeks of vacation each year, your Customer makes $32.50 per hour. In essence, your Customer has to "work" for your company for just over three hours to spend $100. Perhaps the ethic of satisfying exchanges is more evident when we realize that an exchange that fails to deliver value to a Customer steals hours or more of their lives from them. And exchanges that confer surplus on Customers give greater value to the hours of their lives they in effect gave your firm.

Who Has a Stake?

Now we can return to our earlier question about who should be a stakeholder in a company. If our goal is to create the most value possible with society's scarce resources, then only three groups are stakeholders: Customers, Employees, and Owners. Why? Because they are inside "the circle of reciprocity." Only these groups have a direct, reciprocal relationship with the company for mutual benefit. "Direct" and "Reciprocal" are the operative terms here.

Start with the easy case of reciprocity. Thieves and embezzlers are not stakeholders because they take from the company and all of its legitimate partners — but they give nothing back. In fact, we are so offended by their lack of reciprocity that we'll put them in jail if we catch them. Pop quiz: Guided by this decision about thieves and embezzlers, decide if terrorists or trees should be stakeholders. Hint: It's easier to make the case for trees.

"Direct" means that the reciprocal relationship is one where reciprocity between the parties clearly enriches both and does so in rough proportion the contributions of each. No one's sense of reciprocity was satisfied in the Ultimatum game when one player kept $9.99 for themselves and offered only a penny to their partner.

The state generally fails this test because the loop of reciprocity is too diffuse to create truly reciprocal exchange. This is the classic problem with public goods. The benefits of public goods — such as streetlights, national defense, or environmental protection — are shared by everyone whether they helped pay for it or not. So a firm may spend a lot to create the good, but it cannot get paid for it because others will take part in it for free. If a firm, for example, gives to the state by paying to educate all of the high school students near the firm, most of those students will, most likely, work somewhere else, conferring benefits on other companies that take a free ride on the generous firm. In such cases, where a public good — an educated workforce, for instance — is of great benefit to all but which will not be paid for by free riders, the state levies taxes to pay for the good so that taxpayers in general contribute to the goods they receive. If the State does not purchase or create public goods, public goods will be starved for funds and the public at large will suffer. So the firm's obligation, in the case of public goods, is to pay taxes, and to obey public laws and regulations, which should, generally, be crafted to promote the public good.

Are there cases where the relationship between the state and the company is not too diffuse for reciprocity? Yes. The state may be the Customer, in which case the firm is a "government contractor." Or it is also possible and common for the loop between a company and the state to be made tight through lobbying, hiring government Employees' relatives, bribery, etc. This way, the firm is able to divert public resources to create great value for the firm privately, which we call "rank corruption," and that is a crime like thievery, though usually on a larger scale. Except for government contractors – and sometimes even for them – we don't actually <u>want</u> a tight reciprocal relationship between companies and the government because of the access it gives to public resources.

In the case of public goods, the relationship between individual companies and the goals of the state are too diffuse for individual action to produce them. In the case of close seller/Customer relationships between companies and the state, we should be concerned if the relationship is <u>not</u> sufficiently diffuse because public goods can be diverted to enrich private actors.

What if <u>everyone</u> had a stake?

Having dismissed the state as a stakeholder in companies in most circumstances, let me address here the related concept of "Corporate Citizenship" or "Corporate Social Responsibility," abbreviated as CSR. This is a very close cousin of conventional stakeholder theory except that it is often even less clearly defined. The essence of the argument is that corporations, in addition to creating value through their productive activities, should devote some of their resources to promoting the good of society at large.

I'm about to advance a series of arguments that, at best, warrant serious care before a company launches and the public cheers CSR programs. Adherence to the path paved by the CEO Formula does not oppose corporate action in support of public causes as I explain at the end of this section. Nor would it oppose measures that prevent companies from making money by exploiting externalities with, say, the environment, that harm society at large. It does oppose the destruction of value without proof that more value has thereby been created. The CEO Formula and the law should be opposed to attracting investment, Employees, and Customers with shallow and ineffective gestures that dance at the edge of fraud. And the CEO Formula is strongly opposed to the diversion of company resources from the three groups with which a company has reciprocal obligations as well as opportunities without their consent.

Good news and caution about "the good."

Let me begin with one important argument in support of CSR. Many Customers, Employees, and Owners increasingly care about the social consequences of buying from, working for, or investing in certain companies. If one or more of these groups would create more reciprocated surplus with your company if you, say, commit to helping out a local school, then the company is creating surplus for them in doing so. Go for it! That's simple business sense. There is evidence that companies rated highly for their performance on "Environmental, Social, and Governance" ("ESG") scorecards draw more capital at a lower price because trillions of dollars of investment now use ESG as a factor or a screen in choosing investments. And despite all the seeming social intent of ESG practices, they can often be a simple rubric to re-label certain profit-driven undertakings, and some prominent figures have urged companies to pursue profit-driven social impact, or, "shared value" as an ESG strategy.[93] Moreover, the pursuit of goals deemed worthy may be a powerful means to give a company "purpose" beyond pumping up stock values. Employees often prize the purpose of a company, and clear efforts on behalf of causes outside the company's work may inspire them to join and strive at places with otherwise pedestrian ambitions.[94]

---

[93] Michael E. Porter, George Serafeim, and Mark Kramer. "Where ESG Fails." *Institutional Investor* (October 16, 2019), 1. https://www.institutionalinvestor.com/article/b1hm5ghqtxj9s7/Where-ESG-Fails (accessed December 30, 2019).

[94] "Working for socially responsible companies leads to increased organizational identification (Carmeli, Gilat, & Waldman, 2007), employee engagement (Glavas & Piderit, 2009), retention (Jones, 2010), organizational citizenship behavior (OCB; Jones, 2010; Lin,

And yet, caution is warranted.

One, the business case I've just laid out – that Customers, Employees, and Owners may derive value from a company's social stance – is limited to those who create reciprocal value with the company. Delighting far-away moralists does not directly create value and may destroy it by diverting value from C, E, and O. As with the previous discussion of the state as a stakeholder, companies should share value only with those inside the circle of reciprocity. Supplying value to those outside the circle of reciprocity will likely reduce the total amount of social value the firm can create because its distributions would not be proportionately reciprocated.

Two, many CSR advocates point to surveys in which consumers and employees say they feel strongly about the social positions of businesses and that they will spend or work only at firms with whom they agree on such issues. One study reports: "Nearly 90% of the consumers surveyed said they would purchase a product because a company supported an issue they care about. More importantly, roughly 75% will refuse to buy from a company if they learn it supports an issue contrary to their own beliefs."[95]

Many business leaders and CSR advocates cite studies like this to exhibit the imperative for corporate activism without taking note that <u>this cuts both ways</u>! It assumes that all Customers have the same beliefs. If half of a company's Customers <u>disagree</u> with a company's stance, 75% of them – nearly 40% of the customers – may then refuse to buy from that company. An outspoken CEO can only hope that her views are shared by

---

Lyau, Tsai, Chen, & Chiu, 2010; Sully de Luque, Washburn, Waldman, & House, 2008), employee commitment (Maignan et al., 1999), in-role performance (Jones, 2010), employee creative involvement (Glavas & Piderit, 2009), and improved employee relations (Agle et al., 1999; Glavas & Piderit, 2009). In addition, Turban and Greening (1997) found that CSR increases firm attractiveness to prospective employees." Herman Aguinis and Ante Glavas "What We Know and Don't Know About Corporate Social Responsibility: A Review and Research Agenda," *Journal of Management*, 38 July 2012, 947.

[95] *Business News Daily*, April 22, 2019. https://www.businessnewsdaily.com/4679-corporate-social-responsibility.html. (accessed December 4, 2019)

a very large percentage of the population, or she may be seriously damaging a company's success.[96]

How should we define "the good?"

Let's address the more general question: Is CSR, in general, measurably good or bad for business and society at large? Might we be setting up a system where companies' spending on social goods actually destroys more value than it creates?

To answer that, we'd have to know what good "corporate citizenship" or "social responsibility" is. No one seems to be sure. "There is a massive problem around terminology," says Jane Nelson, who directs the Corporate Social Responsibility Initiative at Harvard University. Even when two companies use the same term, "one of them might be looking at [corporate citizenship] much more from a supply-chain management, managing risks, human rights perspective," Dr. Nelson cautions, "whereas another might be, how do we make money out of this?"[97]

Several scholars have proposed definitions of "corporate social responsibility" for other researchers to observe – an example is to define CSR as "context-specific organizational actions and policies that take into account stakeholders' expectations and the triple bottom line of economic, social, and environmental performance," which, without saying what "context-specific" means, or who stakeholders are, or how their expectations should be determined and prioritized, and without specifying what it means to "take into account the triple bottom line"[98]

---

[96] For a detailed and nuanced discussion of the risks and benefits of public CEO activism, see Aaron Chatterji and Michael Toffel, "The New CEO Activists." *Harvard Business Review*, January-February 2018. https://hbr.org/2018/01/the-new-ceo-activists (accessed December 5, 2019).

[97] "Corporate citizenship: Profiting from a sustainable business," *The Economist Intelligence Unit*, 2008, 6.

[98] Aguinis and Glavas, *Journal of Management*, 38 July 2012, 933. The "triple bottom line," originally meant to include the 3 Ps – Profits, People, and the Planet – is not a match with ESG, which is now often

surely adds ambiguity rather than reducing it. I'll discuss the Environmental, Social, Governance or 'ESG'" triple bottom line shortly. The same issues apply there.

In a valiant attempt to be quite specific about what constitutes CSR, the International Standardization Organization – a highly regarded international agency for setting business quality standards – has offered the ISO 26000 guidelines. These contain, depending how you count some of the categories, 60 different social responsibilities for corporations.[99]

---

casually referred to as the triple bottom line. But, of course, ESG omits profits, so it really calls for a quadruple bottom line.

[99] "26000 Guidance on Social Responsibility," International Organization for Standardization, 2018 12-13
https://www.iso.org/files/live/sites/isoorg/files/store/en/PUB100258.pdf
The list of social responsibilities are as follows:
6.2. Organizational governance.
6.3. Human rights, which includes Due diligence, Human rights risk situations, Avoidance of complicity, Resolving grievances, Discrimination and vulnerable groups, Civil and political rights, Economic, social and cultural rights, and Fundamental principles and rights at work.
6.4. Labour practices, which includes Employment and employment relationships, Conditions of work and social protection, Social dialogue, Health and safety at work, and Human development and training in the workplace.
6.5. The environment which includes Prevention of pollution, Sustainable resource use, and Climate change mitigation and adaptation and Protection of the environment, biodiversity and restoration of natural habitats.
6.6. Fair operating practices which includes Anti-corruption, Responsible political involvement, Fair competition, Promoting social responsibility in the value chain, and Respect for property rights.
6.7 Consumer issues, which includes Fair marketing, factual and unbiased information and fair contractual practices, Protecting consumers' health and safety, Sustainable consumption, Consumer service, support, and complaint and dispute resolution, Consumer data protection and privacy, Access to essential services, and Education and awareness.
6.8 Community involvement and development which includes Community involvement, Education and culture, Employment creation and skills development, Technology development and access, Wealth and income creation, Health, and Social investment.

The problem, as ISO surely establishes inadvertently, is that "social responsibility" is an inherently open-ended term. I don't mean to be fussy, but some semblance of precision is critical here to decide whether CSR is good for the financial performance of a corporation and society at large. To do that, researchers would want to compare socially responsible with socially irresponsible corporations. How on Earth would we know, using the ISO 26000 list of 60 responsibilities, whether a given corporation is "socially responsible" if they do a "good job" on 15 of ISO's criteria? On 30? On all of them? Would anyone qualify on the full set? Or what about the researchers' suggested definition cited above, which, while shorter, is entirely vague. <u>The comparisons between responsible and irresponsible companies, as I hope is clear, are themselves irresponsible when the underlying phenomenon of social responsibility is, at best, chaotic.</u> Consider one review of the state of play, including an often-cited "meta-analysis" of other CSR studies:

> Peloza (2009) uncovered that 36 different metrics have been used to assess CSR, and 39 different measures have been used to assess financial performance….Margolis et al. (2009) and Orlitzky et al. (2003) used different sets of primary-level effect sizes in their meta-analyses: Margolis et al. (2009) relied on 192 effects reported in 166 studies, whereas Orlitzky et al. (2003) relied on 388 effects reported in 52 studies.[100]

It should be no surprise that some studies find that CSR improves corporate financial performance, some that it harms it, and some that there is no measurable effect.[101]

---

[100] Aguinis and Glavas, *Journal of Management*, 38 July 2012, 942.

[101] Marc Orlitzky, Frank L. Schmidt, Sara L. Rynes, "Corporate Social and Financial Performance: A Meta- analysis," *Organization Studies*, 24(3): 404, 2003. "The impression that 'in the aggregate, results are inconclusive' regarding any theoretical conclusions about the relationship between CSP and corporate financial performance (CFP) has persisted until today (Jones and Wicks 1999: 212; cf. also Donaldson 1999; McWilliams and Siegel 2001; Roman et al. 1999). Ullmann (1985) and Wood and Jones (1995) argued that during the past three decades of empirical research on this relationship, researchers have engaged in a futile search for stable causal patterns. A number of narrative reviews and theories (for example, Aupperle et al. 1985; Griffin and Mahon 1997; Husted 2000; McWilliams and Siegel 2001; Pava and Krausz 1995; Ullmann 1985; Wartick and Cochran 1985; Wood 1991a, 1991b; Wood and Jones 1995) have proposed conceptual explanations for the existence (or lack thereof) of a causal

One confounding factor, from this book's perspective, is that many studies on CSR's economic effects say that CSR <u>includes</u> providing value to Customers,[102] investing in Employees, and creating value for Owners.[103] KMPG quotes one CEO who explains devotion to environmental, social, and governance issues as reciprocity with C, E, and O!:

> "The founder or CEO recognizes the mutuality principle and determines that <u>the purpose of the company is to create mutuality of services and benefits for all stakeholders – shareholders, employees, customers, and suppliers</u>. Basically the founder or CEO believes that we can only be successful in the long term if everybody we touch is also being successful....So it's not altruism, it's business, and it's a win-win."[104]

In the new Business Roundtable statement on the purpose of business, the 182 signatories "commit to delivering value to our customers....investing in our employees....dealing fairly and ethically with our suppliers....supporting the communities in which we work....and generating long-term value for shareholders."[105] Well, on Customers,

---

relationship between CSP and CFP, but failed to provide clear answers." Note that the authors argue their meta-analysis "suggest[s] that corporate virtue in the form of social responsibility and, to a lesser extent, environmental responsibility is likely to pay off...."

[102] Hafiz Yasir Ali, Muhammad Asrar-ul-Haq, and Rizwan Qaiser Danish, "How corporate social responsibility boosts firm financial performance: The mediating role of corporate image and customer satisfaction," Wiley Online Library, June 10, 2019. https://onlinelibrary.wiley.com/doi/abs/10.1002/csr.1781

[103] "Corporate citizens are accountable not just to shareholders, but also to stakeholders such as employees, consumers, suppliers, local communities and society at large." "Corporate citizenship: Profiting from a sustainable business," *The Economist Intelligence Unit*, 2008, 6.
[104] "The ESG Journey: Lessons from the Boardroom and the C-suite," KMPG, 2018, 5 (emphasis added) https://boardleadership.kpmg.us/relevant-topics/articles/2019/the-esg-journey-lessons-from-the-boardroom-and-c-suite.html (accessed December 4, 2019).

[105] "Business Roundtable Redefines the Purpose of a Corporation to Promote 'An Economy That Serves All Americans'" *The Business*

Employees, and Owners, yes! As I've argued throughout, Customers, Employees, and Owners are special subsets of "society" because they are engaged in creating value with and for the company, and do, in fact, often create significant value if the company handles these relationships properly. One of the five ESG categories is entirely about Employee relations and treatment. But what if the proven value-creating powers of C, E, and O are combined with – drawing from ISO 26000, for example – "Community involvement…and culture [and] Social investment," which could mean opera and symphony performances (as the wealthy often favor) or almost anything else? The effect may be to make species of CSR that are not reciprocated seem as though they do not destroy value because they are combined with actions that do create value.[106]

Roundtable, August 19, 2019. https://www.businessroundtable.org/business-roundtable-redefines-the-purpose-of-a-corporation-to-promote-an-economy-that-serves-all-americans (accessed December 4, 2019).

[105] Taken as a group, socially responsible investments do not improve financial returns. "Despite countless studies, there has never been conclusive evidence that socially responsible screens or company positions on lists such as the Dow Jones Sustainability index deliver alpha [returns greater than the market as a whole]." Porter, Serafeim, and Kramer, 2019, 1. Consider the division between two kinds of ESG practices, material and immaterial. The Sustainability Standards Accounting Board ("SASB"), in addition to its catalog of ESG responsibilities, identifies "material" issues by industry, which "are the issues that are reasonably likely to impact the financial condition or operating performance of a company and therefore are most important to investors." https://www.sasb.org/standards-overview/materiality-map/. One study finds dramatically different performance in stock returns and accounting measures for firms that pursue "material" sustainability investments most important to investors. Mozaffar N. Khan, George Serafeim, and Aaron Yoon. "Corporate Sustainability: First Evidence on Materiality." *Harvard Business School Working Paper*, No. 15-073, March 2015, 3, 12-15. In short, pursuing ESG practices that are most important to investors produces more profits and higher stock returns. Not a shocker.

Who gets to decide what is "good?"

Let me emphasize that the problems with defining and deciding on "social responsibility" or the "public good" are not merely methodological issues for academics; they cut to the core of CSR's ability to accomplish anything. Most folks seem to assume that if we had CSR, companies would do what the advocates of CSR think of as "good." But there is no rule on this. We often have very different and often opposing views of the public good. Some will volunteer to clean up public roads, some will support pro-life or pro-choice efforts, some will press for more demographic diversity in higher education, others will favor more ideological diversity on campus. I'll stop here; this is too obvious. Let me add that the progressive who wants to press the case for CSR should perhaps be reluctant to entrust the choice of CSR projects to an army of businesspeople. (Hell, they say, is answered prayers.)

So, defining "the good" promoted by CSR has not been resolved by academics, international agencies, and others who study it. Unsurprisingly, CSR has the same problem within the company itself.

Who – within a firm – decides which "good" a firm should pursue? Someone will pay for the diversion of money or time into such efforts. Customers may pay with higher prices; Employees may pay with lower wages; Owners, the majority of whom are likely saving for or funding their retirements, may pay with reduced income. Or all three may pay; someone will certainly be "taxed" for these extra-corporate causes. If you accept that Customers, Employees, and Owners are key stakeholders in a company, then you should agree that they deserve a say in how their value may be diluted by a company's own definition of "social responsibility." And, if you accept that gains for any member of CEO can be shared with the others, then if one is "taxed," the others will, eventually, pay. If good Employees leave, Customers and Owners will suffer. If Customers leave, Employees and Owners will suffer. You know the rest. It is no minor matter to choose your causes carefully.

So who should get to decide what to do with the money that would otherwise have gone to the firm's partners in value-creation? Surely we shouldn't ask the C-Suite! In the extreme but not uncommon case, CSR would call for some multi-millionaires or billionaires to divert other people's hard-won resources to their favored cause. Aside from the high odds that the views of the very rich may differ sharply from the rest of a company's stakeholders,[107] there is a striking level of distrust for the C-

---

[107] The charitable deduction is a window on how the wealthy dedicate their spare dollars. "A 2005 analysis by Indiana University's Center on

Suite within companies. "Fortune's CEO Initiative 2019 survey of eleven hundred executives, managers, and employees...." found that "...only 7 percent of employees surveyed said that their leaders often or always exhibit the behaviors of moral leadership."[108]

Maybe we should put it to a vote. Who gets to vote? The Customers, as some consultants recommend?[109] The Employees, as others suggest?[110] One-job, one-vote? Or will votes be weighted by wages so those who will "pay the most get to say the most?" What level of assent will be required? Is 50% and a peppercorn enough to compel contributions from the other 49%? Or should there be a super-majority rule? What if 60% favor a cause and 40% intensely oppose it? Does the intensity of feeling of the 40% matter? Do poorly informed views count? There should be no safety in numbers when it comes to being wrong.[111]

Philanthropy showed that even under the most generous assumptions only about a third of "charitable" giving is targeted to helping poor people. A large portion is allocated to operas, art museums, symphonies, and theaters .... Another portion goes to the elite prep schools and universities that benefactors once attended or want their children to attend." Robert Reich, *Saving Capitalism*, (New York: Alfred A. Knopf) 2015, 147.

[108] Marc Benioff, *Trailblazer, The Power of Business as the Greatest Platform for Change* (New York: Penguin Random House, 2019), 213.

[109] Abeer Raza, "Embracing The Human Element: How Modern Businesses Can Commit To Corporate Social Responsibility," *Forbes, YEC Council Post*, July 16, 2019. https://www.forbes.com/sites/theyec/2019/07/16/embracing-the-human-element-how-modern-businesses-can-commit-to-corporate-social-responsibility/#78ae84cb7eff (accessed December 4, 2019).

[110] Carey Kirkpatrick, "Five Steps To Getting Corporate Social Responsibility Right," *Forbes, YEC Council Post*, July 16, 2019. https://www.forbes.com/sites/forbesagencycouncil/2019/06/21/five-steps-to-getting-corporate-social-responsibility-right/#6f7ba0c73caf (accessed December 4, 2019).

[111] Benioff recounts how many of his employees created "pandemonium" by protesting the sale of that company's products to Customs and Border Patrol because CBP was separating children from their families at the border. "I was confident there had been some misunderstanding; after all, I knew that the services we were providing to CBP weren't being used to separate children at the border." Benioff, 197. Because such internal revolts could cause Salesforce to pull its support from any entity deemed

And what becomes of overruled dissenters? Perhaps they will simply bow to the dominant will of a majority. Or they can always leave if they disagree with the use of wealth they have helped create being used in support of causes with which they disagree. I don't mean to get carried away, but we're already fracturing as a polity because Americans are increasingly moving to places where they will be surrounded by those who agree with them.[112] Should we encourage companies to create further balkanization so that we both live <u>and</u> work with those who think as we do? Neal Stephenson forecast this in his novel *Snow Crash* in 1992, where people select "franchised governments" with different policies in which to live, such as "The Mews of Windsor Heights," or "Mr. Lee's Greater Hong Kong."[113] He only missed on the names, which now include "Texas" and "California."

Just to be clear to those who might yearn for a mirror-place where everyone is like themselves, Stephenson's forecast is *dystopian*.

Measuring effort is not measuring the "good"

A quick word about "impact." Unless CSR and ESG become no more than sound and fury signifying nothing, corporate efforts should be measured also for their actual <u>effects</u>, so we know we are getting something socially valuable with the resources we divert to them. As a former practitioner of public policy, I can assure you that we haven't even begun the struggle until you've tried to compare in common terms the impact of disparate corporate efforts on society. You think <u>defining</u> the good is hard? Wait until you try to <u>measure</u> how much more of it you've produced.

---

unworthy by internal dissent, the company has now created an Office of Ethical and Humane Use to decide such questions. Ibid., 200. Congress often hands such issues to commissions.

[112] Bill Bishop, *The Big Sort: Why the Clustering of Like-Minded America is Tearing Us Apart* (New York: Houghton Mifflin Harcourt, 2009).

[113] Neal Stephenson, *Snow Crash*. (New York: Bantam Books, 1993).

Shortchanging the "good"

But let's simply bracket the problems with defining CSR for study and measurement as well as the hard question about who decides how corporate CSR resources will be channeled. Assume those problems went away and that we live in a place where we all agree on what we'd like companies to spend on outside their businesses. There are still several reasons that companies and the public should be wary of CSR.

First, trying to accomplish social goals through CSR will result in significant under-spending on what would be the optimum level of investment in such goods. This is the result of the eternal free-rider problem. Generous companies will be significantly less devoted to creating things that benefit everyone if others (especially competitors) do not contribute their proportionate share even though they benefit as much as everyone else. Our revulsion against free riders, who take without giving, is a species of the reciprocity instinct, and it is powerful. We hate paying for grifters, and, given a choice, we won't. Private efforts to solve public problems are an unreliable solution because private actors will always under-spend on solving problems that create free benefits to others. CSR is asking only for a new species of philanthropy, which, while helpful, will be far too little to solve significant public problems.

Second, and perhaps worse still, in the context of competitive business, we will end up punishing those who help create public goods. There is no enforcement mechanism to make all firms contribute a fair portion to the public good, so a generous firm's competitors are given an advantage in the marketplace because they don't have to bear the costs of CSR. If a generous firm, say, fills all the potholes in a town and its competitor does nothing comparably expensive, the competitor can lower prices, increase wages, and raise investor returns with the cash they have saved. And the grifter's Employees and trucks will have better roads, thanks to their competitor's efforts.

Some might say that we can call out such grifters to be punished with, say, public shaming. Really? Without some enforced transparency and accounting mechanism to compare the social responsibility of various companies, it is only too easy, as is often the case today, to do pure "public relations window-dressing" to signal virtue at very low cost. Here's a cheap one: Sponsor an annual conference on CSR. It costs very little and will accomplish even less, but it makes for a fine talking point on the company website.

Even the attempts at creating scorecards for measuring aspects of corporate social responsibility do not measure the actual resources a company devotes to its social responsibilities so that could be compared to rivals' efforts.[114] As with CSR, so, too, in ESG, confusion abounds on how to measure actual contribution to social causes. If the ESG movement could create comparable measures of ESG responsibility, this could mitigate the free-rider problem by directing investment, Employees, and Customers away from irresponsible firms.

The problem for ESG scorecards, for now, is the massive ambiguity in defining and measuring a company's efforts in a way that is comparable to other companies. There are, for example, within a randomly selected group of 50 Fortune 500 companies, "20 different ways companies report Employee health and safety data, which leads to significantly different results when looking at the same group of companies."[115] There is no standard method for companies to report ESG data, there is no audit to verify such data as is supplied, and different rating agencies have widely divergent scores.[116] Most disturbing is that "disagreements among ESG data providers are not only large, but actually increase with the quantity of publicly available information."[117] Thus, potential Owners

---

[114] The Environmental, Social, and Governance, "ESG" scorecards, are often designed to identify companies with high risk in these categories, not to compare progress in reaching some concrete standard. And those who use the ESG measurements are overwhelmingly more interested in how a firm treats its shareholders – "governance" – than in, say, carbon reduction or Employee pay. "Governance continues to remain the most important ESG component, as claimed by 86% of respondents." 2019 ESG Survey, *Russell Investments Research*, September 4, 2019, https://russellinvestments.com/us/blog/2019-esg-survey. It can be said that ESG is primarily used as a means to improve the "single bottom line" of profits for Owners.

[115] Sakis Kotsantonis, George Serafeim, "Four Things No One Will Tell You About ESG Data," Journal of Applied Corporate Finance 31 (2), Spring 2019, 53.
https://papers.ssrn.com/sol3/papers.cfm?abstract_id=3420297

[116] Timothy Doyle, "Ratings That Don't Rate: The Subjective World of ESG Ratings Agencies," *American Council on Capital Formation*, (July 19, 2018). http://accf.org/2018/07/19/ratings-that-dont-rate-the-subjective-world-of-esg-ratings-agencies/

[117] Kotsantonis and Serafeim, 61 (incredulous emphasis added).

can easily be misled in to investing in irresponsible firms thought to be virtuous because of their ESG scores.[118]

This difficulty in measuring actual contributions to "the good," however defined, presents the real danger that firms may use CSR to reduce their social obligation to obey laws and regulations. One study found that firms exhibiting high levels of CSR received penalties under the Foreign Corrupt Practices Act 40% lower than otherwise comparable firms.[119] This may undergird the unfortunate explanation for a recent finding about the 181 companies that signed the new Business Roundtable declaration that a corporation's purpose includes duties to its Customers, Employees, and communities, as well as its shareholders. The unfortunate finding was that the 181 corporations who signed, compared to nonsignatory firms from the same industry and of the same size, committed more regulatory violations, bought back more of their shares, had larger market shares (suggesting possible antitrust concerns), and paid CEOs more for weak performance than nonsignatories.[120] The irony is that firms that are socially irresponsible can claim to be on the vanguard of public purposes. Climate progress is an example, where climate advocates may rightly worry that some companies use "greenwashing" claims of environmental responsibility for PR purposes at low cost.[121]

---

[118] "Here's what you need to know about the $12 trillion ESG investment world," Market Watch, December 18, 2019. "This confusion may have also resulted in accusations of mis-selling as investors are surprised by what is held within their ESG-oriented portfolios. In particular, the general public has sometimes been surprised by the inclusion of oil-and-gas companies in ESG-friendly indexes and mutual funds."

[119] "Using prosecutions of the Foreign Corrupt Practices Act (FCPA), we find that more socially responsible firms pay $2.3 million or 40% less than the median fine for bribery." Harrison Hong and Inessa Liskovich, "Crime, Punishment and the Halo Effect of Corporate Social Responsibility," Columbia Graduate School of Business, September 5, 2014. https://www8.gsb.columbia.edu/programs/sites/programs/files/finance/Finance%20Seminar/Fall%202014/Halo.pdf

[120] "Is There Real Virtue Behind the Business Roundtable's Signaling?," *The Wall Street Journal*, December 3, 2019, A15.

[121] "Firms Disagree on Climate," *The Wall Street Journal*, December 12, 2019, B2.

A third limitation on CSR is "diffusion to vapor." Even if every single firm decided to devote itself to CSR, CSR has no agreement on which goods to promote. Go ahead and work up a list of 100 possible goods to be increased by CSR – adult literacy, summer jobs for disadvantaged youth, reduced carbon footprint, homes for abandoned dogs and cats and especially for shivering, pitiful dogs and cats (gets me every time), etc. Or compose a basket of socially responsible goals from the ISO list of 60. I'll guarantee you now that someone will do each. There will be some overlap, but for the most part, CSR efforts will be so diffuse that no dent will be made in any given problem.

We've been working at deciding public issues regarding the creation of public goods for centuries now. Which public goods should we produce and how much should we spend on them? In much of the world, we've settled on the democratic process to do this, deciding in the public sphere which public goods we can tax each other to promote. Not perfect, but it's worked so far. Maybe it has worked only so far, but that's an issue for politics, not business. And if our politics is failing because it is polarized and deadlocked, the last thing we should do is give control over corporate purpose to politicians.

Here, in my humble opinion, is the right answer on CSR. First, because the CEO Formula will directly increase the taxable wealth of companies, Customers, Employees, and Owners, the state can use its taxable share of increased prosperity to provide more public goods. Second, companies can and should support the creation of public goods from which companies and their CEO stakeholders would benefit, but which would be abused by free riders. In helping to create genuine public goods, all of a company's value-creating constituencies should benefit, though they should be carefully consulted first. Therein is a legitimate use of corporate political speech. An excellent example is the public and vocal support by Marc Benioff, the trailblazing CEO of wildly successful Salesforce.com, for a new tax to reduce homelessness in San Francisco.[122] Finally, and, obviously, companies are obligated to pay their taxes and obey the laws in compliance with public decisions to tax and regulate. There is a lot of public benefit to be derived merely from corporate conformance to existing law.

We conclude, therefore, that the list of "stakeholders" is limited to Customers, Employees, and Owners. CEO, not CSR.

---

[122] Benioff, 216-222.

I See Things That Never Were and Say, "Why Not?" And They Say, "Here's Why Not."

If you've agreed with most of my argument so far, and you care about the possibility that your business or all businesses could be far more successful for all of us, you may, as I did, want to run out in the streets shouting "Eureka!" If, like Archimedes, you run in to the street naked while you shout, you don't have to worry about embarrassment – almost no one else is on the street.

It should be clear by now that we know who the stakeholders are and we know that by maximizing the reciprocal relations between them and the company that companies could create far more value. Then why isn't this formula more widely deployed? Why is shareholder primacy still the unspoken rule of business purpose?

I'll review some standard arguments against what I've proposed here. But you'll see that the CEO formula will not work without the hard discipline of accounting and financial statements. Nor will it work without the hard discipline we require in other business decisions. And, this plan will never be adopted if business leaders and managers are being paid to destroy the value of their companies, as many are now.

Business as Applied Science

The first and probably primary reason that the CEO approach hasn't been more widely adopted is that the link between what can be done for Customers and Employees is often far less clear than the link between a cold, hard increase in cash from cost-cutting and the happiness of a firm's Owners. Every dollar saved increases profits by exactly one dollar – in the short run. Lately, many firms have been able to increase the price of their shares without even becoming more cost-efficient – they simply buy some of the company's shares back, reducing the number of shares and thereby increasing the value of the remaining shares. More on this later.

Many business leaders rightly demand to know what creating value for Customers and Employees would mean in business terms as precise as "profits" or "profits per share." And many suspect – sometimes rightly – that an effort to "do more for our Customers" or to "put our people first" is fuzzy-headed moralism or an attempt to hijack the shareholders' duly-earned profits in pursuit of some disguised utopian scheme.

> **Many business leaders rightly demand to know what creating value for Customers and Employees would mean in business terms as precise as "profits" or "profits per share."**

The first answer to this entirely legitimate concern is the rule of reciprocity. Firms are only permitted to create surplus for any group if the firm will receive more surplus in return. One of the core values of The Teaching Company was: "Create fair and lasting relationships with our Customers and our Employees – and expect the same in return." Many companies say something like the first half of that clause; but without the second half – requiring reciprocity – the statement is either deceptive rhetoric or an announcement that the firm is planning to give money away.

But how can we know if a proposal to do something for Customers or Employees will lead to more surplus for them and the firm? The same way we do it for Owners. At the end of the day, business management is an exercise in applied science, and our search as business leaders is one for cause and effect. "How much more of X will lead to how much more of Y?" is the abstract form of almost every meaningful business issue. And yet, a causal equation, $X \rightarrow Y$, consists of a cause, X, and an effect, Y. The results reported in accounting statements are, strictly speaking, only the second half of the equation, the effect. Financial statements are where the score is kept on how much surplus the firm has received in its dealings with stakeholders.[123] But financial statements tell us precious little about what caused the outcomes. They say nothing about how much surplus has been created for Customers or Employees. And they tell us almost nothing about how to create more surplus in the future even for the Owners unless "increase revenue and decrease costs" sounds like actionable advice to you. Do accounting statements tell us anything about whether expanding to new retail locations, or building new factories, or investing more in R&D will lead to greater profits? Hardly. For that, we have to engage in scientific fact-finding and analysis, just as we would in deciding where and how much to invest in Customer or Employee satisfaction.

Moreover, the quest for false comfort from precise answers has led many business leaders to look in the wrong place to create new value. It is so much easier to calculate the value of short-term cost-cutting or debt refinancing or share buybacks that we are often misled into assuming that this is our highest and best use as managers and leaders. That's wrong. Running a spreadsheet is not even a significant part of running a business. And the fixation on that which is most easily quantified will usually lead to the shrinking of soft variables where the greatest successes can be won. Quantification is a beautiful thing, but we have to live with its sometimes easily quantified limitations.

> **Running a spreadsheet is not even a significant part of running a business. And the fixation on that which is most easily quantified will usually lead to the shrinking of soft variables where the greatest successes can be won.**

Finally, I add a caution about precision in the context of creating value for Customers and Employees. The scientific evidence on the value that can be derived from C, E, and O has become voluminous. But rather than fall prey to the ancient error of making the best the enemy of the good, we should probably take another step back and ask just how much precision is needed before getting to work. Given the data on the

---

[123] Which bottom line to use in financial statements is open to debate, but the value of cash flows over time or Economic Value Added ("EVA") are harder to "game" than profits or price per share, and they measure a firm's concrete ability to create and share surplus, since all new value creation will probably be paid for in some part in currency, rather than, say, EBITDA.

shockingly low levels of Customer and Employee surplus created by most firms today – 40% of Employees are disengaged, only 32% of Employees are engaged[124], and the average firm only has 10 to 20% more Customers who would recommend it than those who would not[125] – a protracted debate about precision as a precondition for action is probably causing a drastic loss of value. Measurement, like all business-building, is an iterative process. There is no point in waiting on perfection; you'll never achieve it.

Accounting Precision in Perspective

The second reason many say we don't focus on creating value for anyone but Owners is because that's all that financial statements measure. This myopic focus is a natural outcome – accounting is how business is scored, we've been doing this for centuries, and until accounting can address these other sources of value creation, managers will not be likely to see them. So, on this view, managers are like the fellow looking for his lost keys where the light is best.

What this mocking critique may miss is that there are excellent reasons for the significant role of accounting statements even in a world of reciprocity.

One, Owners' returns matter, and, on my argument here, they matter every bit as much as those received by Employees and Customers. What many who advocate the promotion of the interests of Customers and Employees ignore is that the elevation of those groups should not entail the demotion of Owners. The "CEO" firm should be passionately devoted to all three because it has opportunities and reciprocal obligations with all three.

> **What many who advocate the promotion of the interests of Customers and Employees ignore is that the elevation of those groups should not entail the demotion of Owners.**

---

[124] Amy Adkins, "Employee Engagement in U.S. Stagnant in 2015," *Gallup*, January 13, 2016. A ratio of 1.5:1 is the average ratio of engaged employees to disengaged .

[125] Reichheld and Markey, *The Ultimate Question 2.0*, 42.

Two, bad performance for Owners hurts the other groups. The Kotter and Heskett data suggest that a firm emphasizing Customers and Employees will create less than half as much market value as one emphasizing all three, leaving Customers and Employees – as well as Owners – with less available surplus. Why? First, firms which do not create sufficient value to attract capital from Owners will underperform, wither, or die, which does no good for Customers or Employees. Second, on my argument here, it is likely that some surplus at those firms studied by Kotter and Heskett had been given to Customers and Employees without requiring reciprocated surplus in exchange for it. Finally, if you've run a business with an eye on the bottom line, you know that the hard discipline of cost control, which is central to creating surplus for Owners, can identify waste – no matter which group is being served by an initiative – thereby increasing surplus for all.

I am advocating <u>more</u> accounting. Firms should measure the number, surplus, and profits to the company per Customer. The same for Employees.

In addition to adding two new categories to financial reporting for Customers and Employees, I also propose adding a dimension: the future.

Decisions about the creation of value are almost inevitably about the future; financial statements never are. This vast disjunct between the purpose of a company and the way we keep score calls for the addition of science- and statistics-based accounting: the forecast. Every good business manager or leader has some sort of forecast on which they rely, even if it is only rules-of-thumb kept in a manager's head. I argue for something far more rigorous here. (I do not at all pretend to have discovered something new.[126] Many, many businesses spend great effort forecasting the future. I am proposing that such forecasts include the prospective value of Customer and Employee relationships.)

Because following the CEO Formula requires the Company to constantly decide how to create and receive future reciprocal profits, accounting statements must be understood in a new context. Currently, we do not capture the benefits of forward reciprocity. If a firm has spent millions on benefits for Customers and Employees that the firm expects to produce significant gain in the future through reciprocal exchange, there are only

---

[126] See, e.g., Lev and Gu, *The End of Accounting*. And we must all beware of Warren Buffett's warning that forecasts may reveal more about the forecaster than they do about the future. Buffett, *Berkshire Hathaway Letter to Shareholders*, February 7, 1981 at 8.

two ways to account for that now. One, such spending can be "expensed" as a cost and therefore treated as a dead-weight loss, reducing a firm's reported profits. This will deter such investments.

Or, sometimes more controversially, such forward spending can be "capitalized" – treated as an investment – but the expected returns on the investment will appear nowhere on the financial statements. Capitalized investments in the future will not be punished for reducing current profit on the P&L because capital investments are not accounted as a cost, but may still be regarded negatively because they will reduce immediate cash flows. How often in an investor call do the professional analysts ask how soon and by how much capital expenditures can be reduced? A lot – because they can count precisely that a dollar in reduced "capex" improves cash flow by one dollar. But nothing in the financial statements will show how much reduced capital expenditures could reduce future profits and cash flows.

I appreciate – deeply – that the accounting profession and investors who rely on financial statements do not want unrealized gains "guesstimated" or "SWAGed" into a company's books either because the guesses may be poorly informed or because it affords too many opportunities for fraud. Me neither. But failing to enforce disciplined, science-based forecasts of the future value of Customer, Employee, and capital investments will, as this entire book argues, shrink these "soft variables" to the point where they vanish altogether when they should be the primary purpose of a firm. Such forward-looking statements should be as carefully audited as current statements. Annual reports should be precise in demonstrating the quality of the science and statistics behind their projections.

While the need for accurate reporting is essential, I have seen accountants spend hundreds of dollars of their time arguing about trivial sums without a whit of concern about the future. Mine is an old complaint. But I'm adding this: by disregarding the future value of all investments, firms and investors are dramatically misled if they steer by current accounting. Most folks know this, but we still measure and reward people based on accounting measures developed hundreds of years ago.

Massively Misaligned Incentives

Shareholders, the present-day victors in the ideological struggle for supremacy, have prospered in the past few decades. Conforming to the ideology that shareholders – and perhaps only today's shareholders – come first, most C-Suite Employees at large companies are compensated heavily in shares in the company in order to align management's interests with those of shareholders.

Surely much of shareholders' prosperity in recent decades is the result of invention and diligence, but much is also due to the use of financial devices that can and do damage value-creation. Beginning with a change in SEC rules that made it possible for companies to easily buy their own shares on the market, coupled with low interest rates, and a dramatic rise in executive pay based on share prices, firms have borrowed trillions to buy their own shares off the market since the 1980s, with this reaching a crescendo in recent years. By buying their company's own shares, CEOs and their compatriots have become the most rapidly growing members of the Forbes 400 list of the richest Americans.

Here's the incentive now in place for many high-ranking executives: your pay goes up if the share price goes up.[127] And here's the old-fashioned way to get rich running a company and being paid in stock: you spend the years and effort to build your company; carefully studying and acting on Customer data; equipping your Employees with a strong sense of mission, belonging, and fair treatment; investing in research and development, all the while paying out the sums to your shareholders that remain after you've done those things. After years of such toil, your stock in the company has increased so much in value that the rest of your life will assuredly be prosperous.

Or, instead of all that heavy lifting, you can do some fourth-grade math in an afternoon. The math is this: if a company is making $100 dollars per year in profits and has 100 shares outstanding, profits are $1 per share. If the company borrows $50 to buy up 50 shares, then profits per share on the remaining 50 shares are $2 per share. You have thereby doubled your earnings per share. But isn't squeezing the value out of a corporation and giving it to shareholders as soon as possible the best way to serve them? No.

---

[127] "[T]otal compensation for the 200 CEOs of public firms with a market capitalization of at least $1 billion averaged $22.6 million in 2014. Of this total, we calculate that $16.2 million—72 percent—came in the form of stock awards and buybacks." William A. Galston and Elaine C. Kamarck, "More builders and fewer traders: a growth strategy for the American economy," *The Brookings Institution*, June 2015, https://www.brookings.edu/wp-content/uploads/2016/06/CEPMGlastonKarmarck4.pdf (accessed July 31, 2019).

How much of company profits have gone to shareholders? For the 454 companies listed continuously in the S&P 500 between 2004 and 2013, pathbreaking University of Massachusetts economist William Lazonick found that, excluding the recession years 2001 and 2008, <u>buybacks and dividends taken together have averaged 85 percent of net earnings for all corporations since 1998</u>. The problem is that these kinds of heavy rewards to investors leave only 14 percent for internal investments and compensation increases for workers.[128]

The damage is that companies' investments in themselves and their workers have fallen off dramatically since barriers to share buybacks were dismantled in the early 1980s, as executives have been paid for share price increase, and debt has become much cheaper. A study by Deloitte finds that between the 1980s and today, while the share of GDP dedicated to share buybacks and dividends has increased quickly from roughly 2% to 5.5%, the corresponding share of GDP spent on investment into companies has actually declined: from roughly 10% to 8.5%." Professor Paul Collier offers a different perspective with this finding: "The investment rate of the companies whose shares are traded is 2.7 percent; that of those whose shares are privately held is 9 percent."[129] That's roughly <u>three times</u> more investment in the future if a company does not sell its stock on the open market.

Even among public companies, there are stark differences in research and development spending within industry groups. A 2017 study from McKinsey & Company separated 615 publicly traded companies based on a composite index to determine whether these companies had a short-term (0-2 years) horizon for planning compared to those with a long-term horizon of several years. From 2001-2014, R&D spending at long-term companies increased at an annualized rate of 8.5% versus 3.7% for other companies, so much that by 2014, long-term companies spent 50% more on R&D than others. Over that same period, these long-term companies grew their earnings by 36% more on average than other firms; representing only 27% of the firms studied, they created 44% of growth

---

[128] William Lazonick, "Stock buybacks: From retain-and-reinvest to downsize-and-distribute," *The Brookings Institution* (April 2015), https://www.brookings.edu/wp-content/uploads/2016/06/lazonick.pdf (accessed November 30, 2019).

[129] Paul Collier, *The Future of Capitalism: Facing the New Anxieties* (New York: HarperCollins, 2018), 80.

in total returns to shareholders.¹³⁰ This isn't simply an argument for "long-termism." My point is that the rush to cash out as quickly as possible is killing American capitalism, just as the fixation on shareholders only has greatly diminished our economic potential.

Most noticeably, before shareholder primacy, and executive compensation tied to share price and debt as a means to improve a company's stock price became widespread, workers' compensation rose with their productivity. In fact, from 1948 to 1973, wage and productivity increases were highly correlated: productivity rose 95.7% and wages rose 90.9%. The two parted ways in 1973, dramatically so since the 1980s. Since then, productivity has risen 77%, but wages only 12.4%. Very roughly, if wages and productivity had risen at the same pace as they had done in the past, American wages would be about 50% higher than they are today.¹³¹ If ever the loop of reciprocity were obvious, it is in paying Employees for their increased productivity. The breaking of that merely implicit bond might be a good place to look to uncover the mystery of lower productivity increases in recent decades.

Surely some of the rise in productivity since the 1980s comes from the digitization of work and perhaps old-fashioned increased capital spending, but much also comes from the diligence of the American worker, whose allegiance to capitalism would be more secure if their boats, too, rose with the tide. On my argument here, shared reciprocally, Employees would be far more productive if their boats rose when they themselves raised the tide. The full point is this: not only have workers been undercompensated for their increased productivity, but the economy as a whole may well have suffered because workers would have been more productive had they shared in the gains they produced.

Volumes have been written on the causes of stagnant American wages. Some will surely say that the most significant problem is that low-wage foreign competition keeps wages down. I won't wade into the literature

---

[130] Barton, Manyika, Koller, Palter, and Godsall, "Measuring the Economic Impact of Short-Termism," (McKinsey & Company: February 2017) 1, 6 https://www.mckinsey.com/~/media/mckinsey/featured%20insights/Long%20term%20Capitalism/Where%20companies%20with%20a%20long%20term%20view%20outperform%20their%20peers/MGI-Measuring-the-economic-impact-of-short-termism.ashx. (accessed November 30, 2019).

[131] "The Productivity–Pay Gap," *Economic Policy Institute*, updated August 2018, (accessed July 31, 2019).

here, but consider just the restaurant industry. It is immune to foreign competition – no one goes to Berlin for a burger or to Shanghai for a cup of coffee. Between 2015 and 2017, the restaurant industry has spent 136.5% of its total income on stock buybacks. To fund buybacks, they spend more than they make by borrowing money and dipping into their own cash reserves.[132] Given the arguments in favor of the CEO formula and its case for shared surplus, I find it startling that restaurants give more than all of their profits to just one group – shareholders. Consider what would have happened if they shared all of it with their Employees. McDonalds' could have paid every one of its 1.9 million workers $4000 in higher wages. And that beacon of virtue signaling, Starbucks, could have paid every Employee $7000 more in wages each year.

Many have argued in defense of share buybacks and other means to give a company's wealth to shareholders alone, that a company can reasonably decide that it should distribute available funds – including those that can be borrowed – to the shareholders if there are no other sufficiently worthy uses of the funds. No matter how hard they've looked, so the argument goes, C-suite Employees can't find any product improvements, new products, new means to be more efficient, no way to increase the output and retention of Employees, and they just give up and give the money back to themselves and their shareholders because it is the economically rational thing to do.

The Editorial Board of the Wall Street Journal explicitly made this standard defense of buybacks on March 19, 2019. I'm sure that The Journal simply forgot that their argument defies a law of nature so powerful that much of economics is based on it: Among those truths that all economists hold to be self-evident is that **incentives matter**.

> **I'm sure that The Journal simply forgot that their argument defies a law of nature so powerful that much of economics is based on it: Among those truths that all economists hold to be self-evident is that incentives matter.**

Massive short-term incentives – life-changing amounts of money, riches beyond the dreams of avarice – will matter more than any long-term

---

[132] Katy Milani and Irene Tung, "Curbing Stock Buybacks: A Crucial Step to Raising Worker Pay and Reducing Inequality," *The Roosevelt Institute* (July 2018), https://rooseveltinstitute.org/wp-content/uploads/2018/07/The-Big-Tradeoff-Report_072618.pdf (accessed November 30, 2019).

rewards from hard work over many years. Decisions would be radically different if people weren't being paid for the buyback option. Before buybacks, CEOs invested significantly more in their companies. What has happened in the last 30 years? Did American ingenuity and foresight disappear? Did the business schools all lower their standards for admission? No. A get-rich-quick scheme that actually works was invented. Want proof on top of the mountain of evidence? You've seen it: executives at privately held companies can find three times more places to invest in research and development than their counterparts at public companies who can pay themselves in share-price increases. Even among public companies, those with a long-term plan for value-creation invest 50% more than short-termers. And, while we're at it, the long-termers had a 50% greater chance of being in the top 10% of companies in producing returns to shareholders.[133]

Consider the impact of a much smaller incentive to keep up share price – cost-cutting measures to hit or exceed 90-day earnings targets. Does this incentive, vastly outweighed by the money at stake in a buyback, affect C-Suite decisions? Whatever else we might say about many C-suite Employees, at least a high percentage of Chief Financial Officers are willing to admit that they consciously damage the companies for which they work to produce good-looking reports every 90 days, thereby keeping share prices high and making themselves look like very capable CFOs. In a survey of 400 Chief Financial Officers "80% admitted that they would decrease discretionary spending on R&D, advertising, and maintenance to meet an earnings target. Many CFOs acknowledge that suboptimal maintenance and other spending can be value-destroying. More explicitly, more than half of the CFOs (55.3%) say that they would delay starting a new project to meet an earnings target, even if such a delay entailed a sacrifice in value."[134]

If C-suite occupants will reap millions by deciding to distribute funds to shareholders, including themselves, their decisions about whether to harvest the company today or invest in it for the future will be hopelessly skewed in favor of becoming dramatically more wealthy today. The firm,

---

[133] McKinsey & Company, Measuring the Economic Impact of Short-Termism, 2017, 6

[134] John Graham, Campbell Harvey, and Shiva Rajgopal, "Value Destruction and Financial Reporting Decisions," *Financial Analysts Journal* 62 (September 2006), https://www.jstor.org/stable/4480788?seq=1#page_scan_tab_contents, (accessed August 2, 2019).

its Customers, Employees, future Owners, and the country, all suffer from such transparently rigged decision-making.

Ramming Speed, Scotty!

The final objection to the CEO model is that it surely requires more information and more mental agility to run a firm that works to create value for and from all three groups rather than one, but this objection is simply lazy.

The rule is clear: "The firm should share the surplus received from all of the groups with whichever group or groups will create the most new surplus in exchange for the shared value. The trade is reciprocal – create surplus for the firm, and the firm will create surplus for you." There is one overarching goal: create as much surplus as possible. There are three subsidiary goals that fulfill the primary goal, to create as much reciprocated surplus as possible with Customers, Employees, and Owners so you get richer and so does the world.

A New York Times paraphrase of Einstein put it best: "Everything should be made as simple as possible, but no simpler."[135] To borrow a business metaphor, seek the nearest exit when the pilot announces that on today's flight we'll only worry about speed but not much about and altitude and direction. One-dimensional management is a snare for the simple-minded. In business, there are three kings on the board – protecting and promoting all of them is how to win the game.

---

[135] *The New York Times*, January 8, 1950, cited by http://en.wikiquote.org/wiki/Albert_Einstein. The actual statement by Einstein, and for which we are grateful to Times writer Roger Sessions for having made it simpler in 1950 is, "It can scarcely be denied that the supreme goal of all theory is to make the irreducible basic elements as simple and as few as possible without having to surrender the adequate representation of a single datum of experience."
https://championingscience.com/2019/03/15/everything-should-be-made-as-simple-as-possible-but-no-simpler/

Concluding Thoughts on Who We Become in a World of Reciprocity

Adam Smith taught us that the first rule of the Invisible Hand is to create more value than you consume. Every player in a free market must use their resources to create more value than the resources cost, or the market will take resources away from the provider because cost cannot long exceed the price the market will pay.

The rule of reciprocal profit reveals another imperative: every player must not only <u>create</u> value, but must find profitable ways to <u>share</u> some of it. In a free market, no exchange takes place unless both parties earn surplus, or profit, from the trade. Customers, Employees, and Owners only contribute to the firm in exchange for the expectation that they will receive more from the exchange than they put into it. And the firm follows the same rule; it doesn't deliberately sell to Customers below cost, hire Employees whose compensation exceeds the value they create, or take investments that demand returns greater than the value they can create.

We are all required to create profit for others or they will not create any profit for us. Thus firms that create and share surplus in exchange for surplus will prosper; those that do so with all of their resource contributors will prosper most.

Of course, this does not mean that all successful businesses are virtuous. Forced, fraudulent, monopolistic, and poorly informed transactions are obvious exceptions. It is possible to profit for a time without providing profit to others – Scrooge, Ratbert, Homer Simpson, sub-prime mortgage securities – but, on the argument I've advanced, such profits are unlikely to be sustained and are certain to be less than they could be. Nor does this mean that all "generous" firms will succeed. Without the rule of reciprocity in place, unrequited generosity is a simple road to perdition, paved with good intentions.

If profit-making success means that each actor – on both sides of the transaction – must be careful to bestow value on all with whom they trade, then it is naïve to say that free markets create greed and exploitation. Those who seek short-term gain at the expense of their partners will be continually coached to do better by others with the financial equivalent of a slap in the face: After each trade that is not mutually generous, partners will walk away. Researchers Fehr and Gachter of the Zurich's Institute for Empirical Economic Research find that "the power of reciprocity to shape aggregate outcomes does not only derive from the mere fact that many reciprocal [people] exist. It is also due to the fact that *the existence of reciprocal types changes the behavior of the selfish types.*"[136] In conferring the Nobel Prize in Economics on behavioral economist Richard Thaler, the Nobel Committee reported: "Many individuals are willing to pay a cost (get nothing) in order to punish individuals who made an "unfair" proposal to them, which is a form of negative reciprocity.... Subsequent experiments have shown how the ability and willingness to punish can encourage pro-social behavior."[137] One of the original scholars of reciprocity, sociologist Alvin Gouldner observed, "There is an altruism in egoism, made possible through reciprocity."[138] In time and with understanding, firms, Customers, Employees, and Owners will all be shaped by their desire for gain to care about the welfare of their partners. That understanding and the behavior it entails are both undermined by the doctrine of shareholder supremacy. Thus that doctrine, on my argument in this book, impoverishes firms and the decisionmakers within them both materially and morally.

What sort of persons and groups will emerge from the shaping influences of a system in which a firm's partners must be enriched? We already expect market success to require and create skill, foresight, and industry in the cultivation and transformation of resources or the Invisible Hand will take resources away. In light of the requirement to create mutual prosperity, we should also expect business players to have or acquire skill

---

[136] Fehr and Gachter, Reciprocity and Economics, 848.

[137] The Committee for the Prize in Economic Sciences in Memory of Alfred Nobel, *Richard H. Thaler: Integrating Economics with Psychology*, (Stockholm, October 9, 2017), 21

[138] Alvin Gouldner, "The Norm of Reciprocity: A Preliminary Statement," *American Sociological Review* 25 (April 1960), 173.

in creating prosperity for their economic partners as well as themselves. The "soft" skills of emotional intelligence that allow us insight into ourselves and others aren't fuzzy add-ons for the HR department; they are, along with hard skills in managing resources, data, and timetables, preconditions for flourishing success. Because successful market behavior demands mutually generous reciprocity, markets can transform selfish greed from lead into shared gold.

> **The "soft" skills of emotional intelligence that allow us insight into ourselves and others aren't fuzzy add-ons for the HR department; they are, along with hard skills in managing resources, data, and timetables, preconditions for flourishing success.**

A Case Study: How CEO Worked for Our Company

Creating CEO Goals

During 1996 and 1997, after my awful briefing on the state of my company, and working with about a dozen of my colleagues, we fashioned a plan some 120 pages in length which would carry out the basic principles of the Kotter and Heskett findings. (I plan never to type anything that long again as long as I live.)

Armed with this understanding about the purpose and structure of The Teaching Company, we crafted goals for each of our three key groups, Customers, Employees, and Owners. The goals detailed what value we wanted to create for them and what we wanted from them. I am a believer in Collins & Porras' "Big Hairy Audacious Goals," or BHAGs, and we set them for each group. We published these goals widely within the firm, and, later, included a review of them and the reasons for them in every weekly all-hands meeting. Every Employee had specific objectives and projects to move us toward the goals and was evaluated on them every 90 days. We put it the following way in our annual plan.

> "The Teaching Company is an alliance of shared purpose of three groups: our customers, our people, and our investors. Each of our goals is directed primarily at one of these groups, though in many ways, each goal may benefit more than one group. For our customers, our goal is to ignite the passion for the life of the mind. For our people, our goal is to create great jobs for great people. And, for our investors, our goal is to live long and prosper."
>
> These goals, which are "stretch" objectives, are quantified as follows:
>
> **Customers:** 90% of our customers will rate their satisfaction with our Company, products, and services a 9 or 10 on a 10-point scale. We will have 500,000 customers by 2005, and each of them will spend more than $100 each year with The Teaching Company.
>
> **Owners:** Our return on assets will be over 90% each year—better than the vast majority of companies.
>
> **Employees:** Our people will be as pleased with our company and their jobs as the top 10% of companies. Each of our people should receive sufficient profit shares to invest the maximum amount in our retirement plan, allowing the average TTC associate to retire as a millionaire.

I created a graphic resembling an atom to describe the idea. As a Star Trek fan, I was pleased that the atomic structure of the CEO business was a lithium atom. (The Starship "Enterprise" runs on dilithium crystals.)

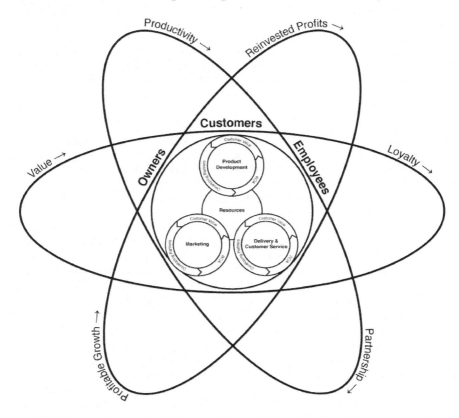

A brief aside on acronyms. As originally crafted, and before I'd heard of the Kotter and Heskett "CEO" findings, I called the three groups Customers, Investors, and People. So we had a "CIP" plan, usually pronounced "chip." The CEO moniker certainly has appeal, but the investors didn't technically "own" the firm any more than shareholders of companies do. And I dislike the term "Employee" because of its impersonality and implicit condescension. "People" felt better in discussing things with my people.

As I said, the goals were BHAGs. Experience has proven to me that if you want to achieve a goal of X, you'd better set a goal of 2X or thereabouts. If

X is your stated goal, everything slows down quite a bit as you approach it. Better to slow down as you nearly double your original hopes.

The "every Employee a millionaire" goal may seem especially extreme. This was partly thinkable because of the strength of our profit-sharing plan, under which the average Employee often received almost $10,000 each year that they could invest and because our workforce was young. I remember pulling out the compound interest tables for a new, 19-year old hire so I could show him the virtues of our plan. If he could produce a 6% return per year, he only needed to save and invest all of his profit shares for less than three years to be a millionaire by 65. Most folks needed to save for longer than that, but the goal was achievable for almost everyone.

There was another route to riches for Employees, our "Value Increase Partner" Plan. That plan granted shares in the value of the company to Employees if the company was sold. Our goal was to make each share worth $100,000. In 2006, when we sold the company, each share was worth $250,000 and one-third of the Employees, some of whom had multiple shares, were "VIPs."

The beauty of profit-shares, retirement plans, and the VIP plan was that we never had to tip-toe around the fact that we were creating value for our investors. I'm often surprised when I talk to other entrepreneurs who don't want to create profit-sharing because they'd have to tell the Employees how much profit the company is making. This is so old school. Tell them, share some, and watch what happens when your Employees who used to be no more than compliant drones pick up the flag and take the hill with it. The better our investors did, the better every Employee at the company did. What we wanted "from" our Employees was to make themselves rich. We ran a modified version of "open book" management. Anyone at the company could know any number in our financials except other people's salaries. And no number could be disclosed to anyone not employed by the company. The policy was strict: I once had the honor to decline to answer customer Alan Greenspan's question about how profitable we were.

Some are thinking, "90% return on assets? Are you nuts?" Well, I said these were Big, Hairy, Audacious Goals. Also, it meant we had three 90% goals: 90% extreme Customer Satisfaction, ratings from our Employees better than 90% of companies, and a 90% return for our investors. What we wanted – and got – from our Owners is that we retained all earnings net of taxes so we could continue to invest in the Company. And we created <u>very high</u> returns on their equity.

Climbing Towards the Goals

Goals are the easy part; then comes the heavy lifting to achieve them. Half of the heavy lift is deciding what to do to achieve them.

It is no longer all that difficult to find out how you are doing at creating surplus in the labor and Customer markets, thanks to the path-breaking work done in the past couple of decades by many scholars and organizations. This much is certain: whether the firm knows how it is doing in creating value for its Customers, Employees, and Owners, every single one of them has a very clear idea of how you are doing. Shouldn't you know as much as they do?

After gathering "bottom line" satisfaction data, and with some more work, a firm can discover those things – in order of importance to each group – that need to be done to move the numbers up. Oddly, in my view, just as the universe likes to arrange things in statistical bell-curves, it also likes to line up problems so that 80% of the problems come from 20% of the causes. Sure, there's variation, but several possible improvements rarely "tie" for equal importance. Knock down the tall bars on the bar chart, survey again, and go after the next batch IF your partners will reciprocate your efforts.

Then, armed with the evidence on how much each of several suggested measures will likely increase the surplus that a given group will give to the firm in exchange for it, a manager can set priorities for investment and action. I don't mean in this quick "how-to" sketch to sound like this is something that happens in an afternoon. My claim is that the pioneers in Customer and Employee research have done much of the work so we can move down the path of measuring and creating priorities for action without having to re-invent the wheel. At my company, we had to invent a lot of wheels. Some did not roll.

Over time, with commitment, measurement and execution improve. You build up a body of Customers whose satisfaction has been quantified, and you can make more precise estimates of the effect of raising satisfaction on any of a number of measures. Another major benefit of focusing on Customer satisfaction is that very satisfied Customers want to help you succeed and will help you figure out how to make your business better.

Extreme Action to Create Extreme Customer Satisfaction

Following the old rule of public opinion research, we started with qualitative work before trying to generate more numbers.

I'll repeat here some of my argument from the main text about how to begin.

There is no "market;" there are people with whom you make exchanges, and understanding the people you serve is the necessary precondition to serving them better.

For your Customers, get up close and invisible. Become the fly on the wall when people talk about your firm. I always had my office next to our call center so I could overhear at least our end of Customer conversations. And, as I've already written, I urge anyone who manages or works in a firm to sit on the other side of a one-way mirror and watch a focus group – or three or four – about the products or services produced by your company. Without them knowing for sure who is listening and watching, let the Customers speak directly about what they think of what you do for a living.

In one year, I sat in on about a dozen focus groups with members of my team. Trust me on this: the experience will make your work life far more tangible to you and, for many, may be a cold splash in the face about things that seemed trivial or merely the concern of your overly-sensitive and unbusiness-like Customer service staff. The experience can be humbling, but it will give the survey results you read a more human and powerful voice. And, yes, your heart may soar when a Customer who loves what you do speaks out. It's an experience you'll want to multiply.

The Teaching Company had been polling Customers to decide which courses to make since 1992. (I mentioned earlier that I worked in government and politics before starting the Company; polling our constituency on what they wanted us to do seemed obvious.) After that, the Company built a robust model allowing it to predict sales, return on investment and even eventual Customer satisfaction with a course based on polling results before the course was ever greenlighted for production. The Company conducted experiments and polls on changes in set design and lighting, use of visual effects, packaging, advertising copy, and so on.

We measured Customer satisfaction on roughly 15 different aspects of the company monthly. Among those were overall satisfaction with the company, likelihood to recommend to a friend, whether the product was worth what the Customer paid, shipping efficiency, Customer service, how knowledgeable our Customer service representatives were about the courses offered, audio quality, etc.

I should note that our profit-sharing plan was team-based, with each part of the company earning applicable Customer satisfaction numbers. What your team earned was multiplied by the percentage of 90% extreme satisfaction the group created. So a group's score in producing extreme Customer satisfaction would raise or lower their profit shares. (Shares <u>within</u> a team were based on individual metrics.) For our recorded teachers and professors, royalties could increase by as much as 50% depending on the score their course earned after a statistically significant number of responses had been gathered. Thus, it was a <u>big deal</u> to get new poll results each month and share them with all of our people at a Friday "Pizza Day" gathering.

We began in the early 1990s with mailed surveys, migrated to phone-based interviews, and then switched to e-mail and web-based surveys. We also received "bounce-back" postcard surveys which were included in every product shipped. Every Customer who responded to a survey received a thank you note. But every Customer who rated the Company less than a 9 or a 10 on any surveyed element was offered a full refund on the product. It is one thing to tell your Customers that you have a lifetime satisfaction guarantee; it is more powerful to write and invite them to invoke it.

This takes a lot of work, but I found the experience exhilarating. Seeing the data on how experiments with Customers, with sales, and with our own people were working delivered much the same thrill that experimenting scientists crave, and I think there is something in our DNA that loves discovery. The often overlooked thrill of business – which is applied science – is that we can generally test our hypotheses more often than scientists can.

A decent rule of thumb would be to book a decade to get all of this right. I'm saying that because it took my company that long. Treat the decade as an outer boundary – new tools are available that we often had to invent; now you can do it in less time. The decade will pass whether you do this or not; you may as well make the best of it.

At The Teaching Company, we raised the proportion of Customers who gave us a 9 or 10 in ratings from roughly 50% to just over 80% in ten years, while increasing the number of Customers by 1000% to 600,000, each of whom spent, on average, $100 per year. By 2006, our "Net Promoter" score was 83.4%, among the best reported by any business, and the company's subsequent growth is in keeping with Reichheld's predictions about such a score. Maybe you think you'll do it in less than ten years: go ahead and do that; it will make my day. Make it a BHAG to do it in 5 years.

Creating a Rich Culture of Custom and Practice for Your People

With absolute protection of the anonymity of their responses, survey your Employees. Read the summary data and the verbatim comments. See what your people think of where they are spending most of the waking hours of their adult lives. After the disastrous review my Employees gave their work-lives in 1996, and after some internal struggle, I embraced the opportunity – and the necessity – to change. This entailed a lot of fumbling around.

We spent years at The Teaching Company trying to create an "Employee satisfaction" measurement tool. The last of our home-brewed surveys asked over 100 questions, and, though we used sophisticated data reduction techniques to hone in on the key issues, the data were murky and inconsistent from year to year. Then I found Gallup's 1999 book, "First, Break All The Rules," in which they described the 12-question instrument they had created over the course of two million Employee surveys. They had built the survey so that the questions were those most linked with the success of the business.

Building on the practices we had in place and now informed by Gallup's data, we held an all-hands meeting every week (coupled with free pizza) to review our goals and our progress in achieving them in each part of the company. We got better and better at this over time. And we'd give applause and awards to teams and people who'd done exceptionally well. In addition, every Employee had a detailed scorecard showing what, quantitatively, they needed to do to move us toward our goals for our Customers, Employees, and Owners. Performance reviews were held every 90 days. This made very clear what was expected of everyone at work, though it required management to labor long and hard to develop and perfect many of the measures we needed to filter this down through the organization and to review them with direct reports every 90 days. But that's not a problem; that's the job.

In detailing these customs and rituals, I don't mean to suggest that money is irrelevant. Base pay must be competitive because that's the measure of whether you are creating as much take-home surplus for an Employee as competitive offers would. Beyond that, I believe the evidence is very strong on the power of profit- or gain-sharing on Employee productivity. We shared 10% of our profits every 90 days.

An individual's effect on company-wide profits is usually too tenuous for a direct incentive effect to matter. I believe that the reason profit-sharing plans succeed is because they send two indirect but clear signals. One, they establish a sense of justice in sharing the fruits of a firm's efforts. People understand this in their bones, and, if handled correctly and implemented honestly, people will respond to surplus-sharing by creating more surplus for the firm. The converse is also true: if the firm is doing well and no one but the C-suite and the Owners seem to be doing better as a result, people will withhold their best efforts since those efforts won't be reciprocated.

Next, I believe that profit-sharing gives cost-control traction at every level of the firm. Everyone "gets" that a dollar in reduced expense increases profits by exactly one dollar. I recall overhearing an old hand who worked in our warehouse chewing out a new Employee who had used five paper towels to dry his hands: "You only need two to do that – the others come right out of my profit share!"

One goal for our Employees was to be rated more highly than 90% of other firms in widely conducted surveys. In 2006, after a decade of effort, the Hay Group surveyed our people using the instrument they had developed and deployed with thousands of firms. We asked to be benchmarked against the top 10% of companies on each of their 57 measures: we were in the top 10% on 38 of them, and I suspect that far fewer than 10% of firms were in the top 10% so consistently.

What reciprocal result did we want from our Employees? As I noted before, we wanted the firm to generate sufficient profit-shares that the average Employee would be able to retire as a millionaire if they invested their profit shares. This nicely coupled our Owners' and Employees' interests.

These weren't feel-good goals: Our revenues and profits per Employee were far better than any public company in the publishing industry – profits per employee were three times the industry average and more than a third higher than the best score from public companies. From 1996 to 2000, our profits rose 230%. From 2000 to 2006 they rose another 300%. With almost no debt, our return on equity from 1999 until my partners and I sold the firm in 2006 was over 50% every year.[139]

---

[139] For the more technically oriented, our five-year Compound Annual Growth Rate (CAGR) in Revenue in 2006 was 14.4%; in EBITDA, the CAGR was 20.9%. The return to our partners when the company was sold was 90 times their original investment.

All This and You're Still in Kansas? Right?

One might say, in light of these results, that all of this has been a long way around to prove that all I'm advocating here is maximizing the gain to Owners, and that we've simply discovered that the best way to do that, in the long run, is to increase returns to Customers and Employees. Maybe this has all been a long trip from Kansas to Oz, only to end up happy in Kansas again.

No.

I'll repeat here from the main text:

The CEO Formula's departure from shareholder primacy is this:

> 3) A company's purpose is not to maximize profits for its Owners.
>
> 4) <u>A company's purpose is to create maximum mutual profit with Customers, Employees, and Owners and to recycle the company's share from those exchanges to do more of the same.</u>

Restated differently as universal goals in practice:

- Make world-class, insanely great products and services – even extrusion nozzles – for Customers who will buy repeatedly and profitably;
- Help your Employees build great lives with the work they do and the profits they create through productive and inventive effort; and
- Protect and grow for the long run the savings Owners have entrusted to you.

Why did I wait so long to write this?

Actually, I started writing this in 1996 during my monastic seclusion with a pile of articles, case studies, and books. At the time, I wasn't sure this would work, and, if it did, I wanted to keep it a secret from our competitors. I sold almost all of my interest in The Teaching Company, now doing business as The Great Courses, in 2006. I served on the Board until 2011. Only recently did my confidentiality agreement with the company expire, allowing me to tell the story of what we did and why.

OK, life got in the way, too. And life is good, but I will, all my life, recall the beautiful decade from 1996-2006, a "Golden Age," when I worked with a group of talented and devoted people to take advantage of something few ever have – the opportunity to build the place where we worked.

A sage once said the only thing in this life you give that is more sacred than your love is your labor. And we were able to build a place for our labor that created not just value, but joy, for ourselves, for hundreds of thousands of our Customers, for hundreds of our colleagues, and for a dozen very loyal investors.

Bibliography

Abowd, John. "The Effect of Wage Bargains on the Stock Market Value of the Firm." *The American Economic Review* 79 (1989). http://www.jstor.org/stable/1827932 (accessed November 30, 2019).

Adkins, Amy. "Employee Engagement in U.S. Stagnant in 2015." *Gallup*, (January 13, 2016).

Aguinis, Herman and Glavas, Ante "What We Know and Don't Know About Corporate Social Responsibility: A Review and Research Agenda," *Journal of Management*, 38 July 2012 932-968.

Ali, Hafiz Yasir, Asrar-ul-Haq, Muhammad, and Danish, Rizwan Qaiser, "How corporate social responsibility boosts firm financial performance: The mediating role of corporate image and customer satisfaction," Wiley Online Library, June 10, 2019.
https://onlinelibrary.wiley.com/doi/abs/10.1002/csr.1781

Axelrod, Robert. *The Evolution of Cooperation*. New York: Basic Books, 2006.

Aydintan, Belgin and Hakan Koç. "The Relationship between Job Satisfaction and Life Satisfaction: An Empirical Study on Teachers." *International Journal of Business and Social Science* 10 (October 2016). https://www.researchgate.net/publication/314261752_The_Relationship_between_Job_Satisfaction_and_Life_Satisfaction_An_Empirical_Study_on_Teachers (accessed November 30, 2019).

Baumhart, Raymond C. "How Ethical are Businessmen?" *Harvard Business Review* (July-August 1961).

Barton, Dominic et al., "Measuring the Economic Impact of Short-Termism." *McKinsey & Company,* February 2017. https://www.mckinsey.com/~/media/mckinsey/featured%20insights/Long%20term%20Capitalism/Where%20companies%20with%20a%20long%20term%20view%20outperform%20their%20peers/MGI-Measuring-the-economic-impact-of-short-termism.ashx (accessed November 30, 2019).

Becker, Howard. *Man in Reciprocity: Introductory Lectures on Culture, Society and Personality.* Santa Barbara, CA: Greenwood Publishing, 1973.

Benioff, Marc. *Trailblazer, The Power of Business as the Greatest Platform for Change.* New York: Penguin Random House, 2019.

Besanko, David, David Dranove, and Mark Shanley. "Competitive Advantage and Value Creation: Analytical Tools and Conceptual Foundations." *The Economics of Strategy.* New York: John Wiley & Sons, 1996.

Bishop, Bill, *The Big Sort: Why the Clustering of Like-Minded America is Tearing Us Apart* (New York: Houghton Mifflin Harcourt, 2009).

Buckingham, Marcus and Curt Coffman. First, Break All the Rules: What the World's Greatest Managers Do Differently. New York: Simon & Schuster, 1999.

Buffett, Warren. *Berkshire Hathaway Letter to Shareholders*, February 7, 1981.

Chamberlain, Andrew. "Does Company Culture Pay Off? Analyzing Stock Performance of 'Best Places to Work' Companies." *Glassdoor.* (March 2015).

Chatterji, Aaron and Toffel, Michael, "The New CEO Activists." *Harvard Business Review*, January-February 2018. https://hbr.org/2018/01/the-new-ceo-activists. (accessed December 5, 2019)

Cialdini, Robert P. *Influence: The Psychology of Persuasion.* New York: HarperCollins, 2007.

Collier, Paul. *The Future of Capitalism: Facing the New Anxieties.* New York: HarperCollins, 2018.

Collins, James and Jerry Porras. *Built to Last: Successful Habits of Visionary Companies.* New York: Harper Collins Publishers, 1994.

Collins, James. "21st Century Start-Up," *Inc. Magazine*, (October 1997).

Committee for the Prize in Economic Sciences in Memory of Alfred Nobel. *Richard H. Thaler: Integrating Economics with Psychology*. Stockholm: October 9, 2017.

Deschamps, Jean-Phillippe and Ranganath Nayak. *Product Juggernauts: How Companies Mobilize to Generate a Stream of Market Winners*. Boston, MA: Harvard Business School Press, 1995.

Doyle, Timothy. "Ratings That Don't Rate: The Subjective World of ESG Ratings Agencies," *American Council on Capital Formation*, (July 19, 2018). http://accf.org/2018/07/19/ratings-that-dont-rate-the-subjective-world-of-esg-ratings-agencies/

Drucker, Peter F. *The Frontiers of Management*. Abingdon, United Kingdom: Routledge, Reprint 2012.

Edmans, Alex. "28 Years of Stock Market Data Shows a Link Between Employee Satisfaction and Long-Term Value." *Harvard Business Review*, (March 2016).

Eklof, Jan, Olga Podkorytova, and Aleksandra Malova. "Linking Customer satisfaction with financial performance: an empirical study of Scandinavian banks." *Total Quality Management & Business Excellence* 29. (August 2018).

Fehr, Ernest and Simon Gachter. "Reciprocity and Economics: The economic implications of *Homo Reciprocans*." *European Economic Review* 42. Amsterdam: Elsevier Science, 1998.

Fornell, Claes, Forrest Morgeson, and Tomas Hult. "Companies that do better by their customers also do better in the stock market." *LSE Business Review*, (February 2017).

Freeman, R. Edward. *Strategic Management: A Stakeholder Approach*. Cambridge, United Kingdom: Cambridge University Press, 2010.

Frey, Phyllis and Martin Frey. *Contract Law*. Boston, MA: Cengage, 2001.

Gale, Bradley and Robert Wood. *Managing Customer Value*. New York, NY: Free Press, 1994.

Galston, William A. and Elaine C. Kamarck. "More builders and fewer traders: a growth strategy for the American economy." *The Brookings Institution,* June 2015. https://www.brookings.edu/wp-content/uploads/2016/06/CEPMGlastonKarmarck4.pdf (accessed November 30, 2019).

Gordon, Jeffrey. "The Rise of Independent Directors in the United States, 1950-2005: Of Shareholder Value and Stock Market Prices." *Stanford Law Review* 59, https://www.jstor.org/stable/40040395 (accessed November 30, 2019).

Gouldner, Alvin. "The Norm of Reciprocity: A Preliminary Statement." *American Sociological Review* 25 (April 1960).

Graham, John, Campbell Harvey, and Shiva Rajgopal. "Value Destruction and Financial Reporting Decisions." *Financial Analysts Journal* 62 (September 2006).

Gramm, Phil and Solon, Mike. "Warren's Assault on Retiree Wealth." *The Wall Street Journal*, September 10, 2019, https://www.wsj.com/articles/warrens-assault-on-retiree-wealth-11568155283 (accessed November 30, 2019).

Harrison, Jeffrey and Douglas, Bosse. "How much is too much? The limits to generous treatment of stakeholders." *Business Horizons* 56 (May 2013).

Hart, Christopher W. "Beating the Market with Customer Satisfaction." *Harvard Business Review* (March 2007).

Hakanen, Jari and Wilmar Schaufeli. "Do burnout and work engagement predict depressive symptoms and life satisfaction? A three-wave seven-year prospective study," *Journal of Affective Disorders* 141 (December 10, 2012). https://www.sciencedirect.com/science/article/abs/pii/S0165032712001966 (accessed November 30, 2019).

Heskett, James, et al. "Putting the Service-Profit Chain to Work." *Harvard Business Review*, (March-April 1994).

Hobhouse, Leonard. *Morals in Evolution: A Study in Comparative Ethics (Classic Reprint)*. London, United Kingdom: Forgotten Books, 2017.

Hoffman, Elizabeth, Kevin McCabe and Vernon Smith. "Behavioral Foundations of Reciprocity: Experimental Economics and Evolutionary Biology." *Economic Inquiry* 36 (July 1998).

Hong, Harrison and Inessa Liskovich, "Crime, Punishment and the Halo Effect of Corporate Social Responsibility," Columbia Graduate School of Business, September 5, 2014.

International Organization for Standardization, "26000 Guidance on Social Responsibility" 2018. https://www.iso.org/files/live/sites/isoorg/files/store/en/PUB100258.pdf

Jensen, Michael C. "Value Maximization, Stakeholder Theory, and the Corporate Objective Function," *Journal of Applied Corporate Finance*, Fall 2001

Khan, Mozaffar N., George Serafeim, and Aaron Yoon. "Corporate Sustainability: First Evidence on Materiality." *Harvard Business School Working Paper*, No. 15-073, March 2015.

Kiechel, Walter. "The Management Century." *Harvard Business Review* (November 2012), https://hbr.org/2012/11/the-management-century (accessed November 30, 2019).

Kirkpatrick, Carey, "Five Steps To Getting Corporate Social Responsibility Right," *Forbes, YEC Council Post*, July 16, 2019. https://www.forbes.com/sites/forbesagencycouncil/2019/06/21/five-steps-to-getting-corporate-social-responsibility-right/#6f7ba0c73caf. (accessed December 4, 2019).

Kotsantonis, Sakis and George Serafeim, "Four Things No One Will Tell You About ESG Data," Journal of Applied Corporate Finance 31 (2), Spring 2019. https://papers.ssrn.com/sol3/papers.cfm?abstract_id=3420297

Kotter, John and James Heskett. *Corporate Culture and Performance*. New York: Free Press, 1992.

Lazonick, William. "Stock buybacks: From retain-and-reinvest to downsize-and-distribute." *The Brookings Institution* (April 2015), https://www.brookings.edu/wp-content/uploads/2016/06/lazonick.pdf (accessed November 30, 2019).

Leakey, Richard and Roger Lewin. *The People of the Lake*. Glasgow: Avon Books, 1978.

Leo, David and Craig Cmiel. *The Financial Advisor's Success Manual.* New York: AMACOM, 2017.

Lev, Baruch and Feng Gu. *The End of Accounting and the Path Forward for Investors and Managers.* Hoboken, New Jersey: Wiley Finance Series, 2016.

Martin, Roger. "The Age of Customer Capitalism." *Harvard Business Review* (January-February 2010) https://hbr.org/2010/01/the-age-of-customer-capitalism (accessed November 30, 2019).

McKinnon, Ronald I. *The Order of Economic Liberalization.* Baltimore: Johns Hopkins University Press, 1993.

Micklethwait, John and Adrian Wooldridge. *The Company: A Short History of a Revolutionary Idea.* London: Orion Publishing Group, 2005.

Milani, Katy and Irene Tung. "Curbing Stock Buybacks: A Crucial Step to Raising Worker Pay and Reducing Inequality." *The Roosevelt Institute* (July 2018), https://rooseveltinstitute.org/wp-content/uploads/2018/07/The-Big-Tradeoff-Report_072618.pdf (accessed November 30, 2019).

Mitchell, Ronald K., Bradley R. Agle, and Donna J. Wood. "Toward a Theory of Stakeholder Identification and Salience: Defining the Principle of Who and What Really Counts." *The Academy of Management Review* 22 (1997).

Naz, Summira. "Relationship of Life Satisfaction and Job Satisfaction among Pakistani Army Soldiers." *Journal of Business Research* 1 (2015).

Orlitzky, Marc, Schmidt Frank L., and Rynes Sara L., "Corporate Social and Financial Performance: A Meta- analysis," *Organization Studies*, 24(3): 404, 2003

Pfeffer, Jeffrey. *Competitive Advantage Through People: Unleashing the Power of the Workforce.* Cambridge: Harvard Business School Press, 1994.

Piaget, Jean. *The Moral Judgment of the Child.* New York: Simon and Schuster, 1997.

Pinker, Steven. *Enlightenment Now: The Case for Reason, Science, Humanism, and Progress.* London: Penguin Books, 2019.

Michael E. Porter, George Serafeim, and Mark Kramer. "Where ESG Fails." *Institutional Investor* (October 16, 2019). https://www.institutionalinvestor.com/article/b1hm5ghqtxj9s7/Where-ESG-Fails
(accessed December 30, 2019)

"The Productivity–Pay Gap." *Economic Policy Institute.* https://www.epi.org/productivity-pay-gap/ (accessed November 30, 2019).

Raza, Abeer, "Embracing The Human Element: How Modern Businesses Can Commit To Corporate Social Responsibility," *Forbes, YEC Council Post,* July 16, 2019.
https://www.forbes.com/sites/theyec/2019/07/16/embracing-the-human-element-how-modern-businesses-can-commit-to-corporate-social-responsibility/#78ae84cb7eff (accessed December 4, 2019)

Reich, Robert, *Saving Capitalism*, (New York: Alfred A. Knopf) 2015.

Reichheld, Frederick F. and Rob Markey. *The Ultimate Question 2.0 (Revised and Expanded Edition): How Net Promoter Companies Thrive in a Customer-Driven World.* Boston: Harvard Business School Press, 2011.

Reichheld, Frederick F. and W. Earl Sasser, Jr. "Zero Defections: Quality Comes to Services." *Harvard Business Review* (September-October 1990).

Reichheld, Frederick. *Loyalty Rules!: How Today's Leaders Build Lasting Relationships.* Boston: Harvard Business School Press, 2003.

Reichheld, Frederick. *The Loyalty Effect: The Hidden Force Behind Growth, Profits, and Lasting Value.* Boston: Harvard Business School Press, 1996.

Robinson, Daniel. "Aristotle on the Knowable." *The Great Ideas of Philosophy, Part II, Lecture* 12 (Chantilly, Virginia, The Teaching Company, 1997).

Russell Investments Research, 2019 ESG Survey, September 4, 2019. https://russellinvestments.com/us/blog/2019-esg-survey.

Mitchell, Ronald K., Bradley R. Agle, and Donna J. Wood. "Toward a Theory of Stakeholder Identification and Salience: Defining the Principle of Who and What Really Counts." *The Academy of Management Review* 22 (1997).

Seppälä, Emma and Kim Cameron. "Proof That Positive Work Cultures Are More Productive." *Harvard Business Review* (December 2015), https://hbr.org/2015/12/proof-that-positive-work-cultures-are-more-productive (accessed November 30, 2019).

Starik, Mark. "Should Trees Have Managerial Standing? Toward Shareholder Status for Nonhuman Nature." *Journal of Business Ethics* 14 (March 1995).

Stephenson, Neal. *Snow Crash*. (New York: Bantam Books, 1993).

Stevens, Scott P. *Games People Play: Game Theory in Life, Business, and Beyond* (Chantilly, Virginia: The Teaching Company, 2008).

Stout, Lynn. *The Shareholder Value Myth: How Putting Shareholders First Harms Investors, Corporations, and the Public*. San Francisco: Berrett-Koehler, 2013.

Thurnwald, Richard. "Economics in Primitive Communities." *The Annals of the American Academy of Political and Social Science*, 1 (March 1934).

Unocal Corp. v. Mesa Petroleum Co., 493 A.2d 946 (Del. 1985)

Warren, Elizabeth. "Issues." https://elizabethwarren.com/issues#rebuild-the-middle-class (accessed August 2, 2019).

Wheelan, Charles. *Naked Money: A Revealing Look at What It Is and Why It Matters*. New York: W.W. Norton, 2016.

Wilson, James Q. *The Moral Sense*. New York: Free Press, 1997.

About the Author

After graduating from Georgetown University with a B.A. degree in philosophy, Tom was voted the nation's "Outstanding College Debater of the Decade of the 1970's." Tom attended Harvard Law School where he served as an editor of the Harvard Law Review, graduating *magna cum laude*.

Tom then clerked for the Honorable James L. Oakes of the United States Court of Appeals for the Second Circuit, going on to practice law as a litigator with the Houston firm of Susman Godfrey.

In 1985, Tom became Chief of Staff and Chief Counsel to the United States Senate Committee on Labor and Human Resources, chaired by Edward M. Kennedy (D. Mass.), which enjoyed a broad jurisdiction over domestic policy, including federal education spending.

In 1989, Tom left government service to found The Teaching Company, which recruits the country's best university, college, and high school teachers, records their lectures in audio and video, and sells these recordings to the public. The Company has been described by The New York Times as "a force in continuing education" and by The Wall Street Journal as "the colossus of its field." Tom served as CEO and Chairman until he sold most of his interest in 2006; he served as one of its Directors until 2011.

Tom is married to law school classmate, Victoria Radd Rollins. They live in McLean, Virginia. Tom supports debate programs at Georgetown University and through the National Urban Debate League. He received the National Speech and Debate Association's Alumni Lifetime Achievement Award in 2015. He is also the 2012 recipient of the American Council of Trustees and Alumni Merrill Award for promotion of the liberal arts. He has set two Virginia state weightlifting records in the bench press, and won the 2011 competitive shotgunning "A Class" World Championship at the World English Sporting Clays tournament.

Made in the USA
Middletown, DE
15 June 2020